POETRY of RESISTANCE

Camino del Sol
A Latina and Latino Literary Series

POETRY of RESISTANCE

VOICES FOR SOCIAL JUSTICE

Edited by
FRANCISCO X. ALARCÓN
AND ODILIA GALVÁN RODRÍGUEZ

Foreword by
JUAN FELIPE HERRERA

THE UNIVERSITY OF
ARIZONA PRESS

TUCSON

The University of Arizona Press
www.uapress.arizona.edu

Printed in the United States of America
21   20   19   18   17   16   6   5   4   3   2   1

ISBN-13: 978-0-8165-0279-0 (paper)

Cover design by Leigh McDonald
Cover illustration by Porter McDonald

Francisco X. Alarcón's "Para Los Nueve del Capitolio / For the Capitol Nine" appears in
Borderless Butterflies / Mariposas sin fronteras (Poetic Matrix Press, 2014). "Niño traga fuegos"
by Elizabeth Cazessús is from her book *Hijas de la ira* (Nódulo Ediciones, 2013). "Trespasser
Shoes" by César Love has appeared in *Haight Ashbury Literary Journal, Somos en escrito, In
Other Words,* and *The Merida Review.* Richard Vargas's poem "For a Friend Who Objects
to Comparing the Events Leading Up to the Holocaust with What Is Happening Today in
Arizona" originally appears in his poetry collection *Guernica, revisited* (Press 53, 2014). Alma
Luz Villanueva's "Breathing While Brown" appears in *GRACIAS* (Wings Press, 2015).

Publication of this book is made possible in part by the proceeds of a permanent endowment
created with the assistance of a Challenge Grant from the National Endowment for the
Humanities, a federal agency.

Library of Congress Cataloging-in-Publication Data
Poetry of resistance : voices for social justice / Edited by Francisco X. Alarcón and Odilia
Galván Rodríguez ; foreword by Juan Felipe Herrera.
    pages cm. — (Camino del sol : a Latina and Latino literary series)
  Chiefly in English with several poems in Spanish; some poems in English and Spanish, and
one poem in Irish.
  ISBN 978-0-8165-0279-0 (pbk. : alk. paper)
  1. Arizona—Emigration and immigration—Poetry. 2. Hispanic Americans—Arizona—
Poetry. 3. Protest poetry, Spanish American. I. Alarcón, Francisco X., 1954– editor. II.
Galván Rodríguez, Odilia, editor. III. Herrera, Juan Felipe, writer of foreword. IV. Series:
Camino del sol.
  PS595.E54P64 2016
  811'.60809791—dc23
                              2015023995

∞ This paper meets the requirements of ANSI/NISO Z39.48-1992 (Permanence of Paper).

CONTENTS

FOREWORD

They Carry Butterflies in Their Hands

It is raining. The pickup slams and careens through the Mojave. There is a blast of bullets. Innocents go down. There's a chant to the corn goddess. A man kisses his father's hand, the father who worked for him all his life and never expected anything back. And there are bulldozers, abrazos, and silence. You heart must be polished to continue. Border dogs on leashes are snapping at your child's shoulder in your own home. Marigolds appear across that ancient migration route. Turtle Island holds onto you. Something rooted from your heart down to the red bones of earth sustains you—petals, cottonwoods, sagebrush. The fragrance of *xocolatl*—then a baton. All the names come out of you. You return, somehow, to your land. It is yours because it knows you—intimately.

To write the first paragraph, I gathered words from the verse of the eighty-eight poets in this magnificent collection. You can sense the unity of the voices and the bitter honey of their songs—across time, terrain, family, loss, brutality, and transcendence. Against all odds, each one, from various cultural places, holds hands with the other. The poems—even in their poetic form—stand tall. They are calls to ancient deities and day-to-day families. Along the way there are stops, sacred visions, and a deep acknowledgment of the severe tasks of resistance, that is, marching, witnessing, and facing death and pointed, armed, and fanged beings with compact orders to attack.

Susan Deer Cloud asks, "Will you ever know how it feels to love . . . ?" Nancy Aidé González notices "La Virgen de las Calles . . . / full of yearning." It is in this manner that each poem severs border wires and installations in whatever shapes and materials they may appear. Borders can be overcome with the revolutionary tenderness of poems en Resistencia. Listen: "I am the dew on the cool morning," says Hedy García Treviño. Jabez W. Churchill envisions a trek of "five hundred miles of taquerias." How can suffering and ill-shaped laws be overcome? Listen, listen to Jorge Tetl Argueta speak of the children—"They carry butterflies in their hands."

This anthology, *Poetry of Resistance*, edited by Francisco X. Alarcón and Odilia Galván Rodríguez, is an incredible assemblage of voices and letters that proves that collective poetry is the answer to the violence-filled policies that increasingly face us in these times.

Open this book of leaves if you do not believe me.

Juan Felipe Herrera
U.S. Poet Laureate

INTRODUCTION

On April 20, 2010, nine Latino students chained themselves to the main doors of the Arizona State Capitol in Phoenix in an act of civil disobedience to protest the passage of Arizona's "reasonable suspicion" law, SB 1070. This law legalizes racial profiling and police abuse against people "suspected" of being in the United States without papers.

That same day Professor Francisco X. Alarcón of the University of California, Davis, received an urgent e-mail message from Professor Manuel de Jesús Hernández of Arizona State University, including a link to a YouTube video of the nonviolent direct action protest against SB 1070 and the subsequent arrest of nine young Latino students.

Moved by the courageous actions of these young students, reminiscent of Dr. Martin Luther King Jr. and Mahatma Gandhi in their struggles for civil rights and independence from colonialism, Professor Alarcón responded immediately by writing a poem in Spanish and English titled "Para Los Nueve del Capitolio / For the Capitol Nine," dedicated to the students. The poem was e-mailed to Professor Hernández, who managed to get it to the jailed students. The students read the poem and responded with a collective online message in gratitude.

With a desire to share what was taking place with the widest possible audience, Professor Alarcón created a Facebook page called "Poets Responding to SB 1070" and posted the poem he had dedicated to the students, now the first poem in this anthology.

After the creation of the new Facebook page, many poets and other people responded immediately by commenting on the poem and the action taken by the students in Phoenix. Poets Alma Luz Villanueva and Antoinette Nora Claypoole offered their assistance. Professor Alarcón invited other poets to join him as moderators of the page, among them poet/activist Odilia Galván Rodríguez.

This Facebook page was created to encourage poets, writers, artists, activists, and the general public to respond to and keep informed about the challenges of this historically racist legislation. Shortly after its inception, SB 1070 was followed by HB 2281, a law that bans ethnic studies in Arizona high schools, targeting Chicano/a studies in the Tucson Unified School District.

The poet-moderators called on other people to lift their voices, to engage in nonviolent direct action campaigns, and to form challenges to any and all upcoming copycat laws being proposed in other states. Hundreds of poems from all over the United States and the world were soon posted on the Facebook page. *Poetry of Resistance: Voices for Social Justice* is a reflection of this collective poetry project and of the power of the word.

"Poets Responding to SB 1070" has been in existence since the end of April 2010, and from its inception, it has gained tremendous momentum and become an open forum where poetics and politics engage in exciting and groundbreaking new ways. While we were a bit surprised by the overwhelming success it has become, we know that poetry is powerful and that combining poetics and art with activism is something that moves people more than traditional organizing does and generates enthusiasm.

"Poets Responding to SB 1070" calls on poets, in a much deeper way than previously, to be not only artists but also activists and to act in solidarity with a cause; it has become a true poetic movement. We have participation from a multigenerational and multilingual group of poets who have diverse ethnic backgrounds and who come from diverse political affiliations and from many regions of the globe. What unites us is our commitment to express solidarity and support for a humane, just, and comprehensive immigration reform in the United States. We advocate civil and human rights for all, without distinction of legal status in this country.

More than 3,000 original poems have been submitted and posted to the Facebook page, which had received, at the end of 2014, more than 8,400 "likes" (or participants) and at times more than 600,000 "hits" (or views). It is not rare for the page to have more that 40,000 hits in a single week. We are always on the lookout for up-to-the minute articles that feature the issues and themes of our page to share with our readers. It is also not unusual for us to get more than 5,000 hits on one article, as in the case of a story about the Central American refugee children fleeing oppression in their countries. In many regards, "Poets Responding to SB 1070," as part of social media, represents a return to the oral tradition in which "storytellers/writers" engage "listeners/readers" in a direct way to reflect and act.

During the past four years the moderators, chiefly Francisco X. Alarcón and Odilia Galván Rodríguez, have spoken on these issues at several national conferences, such as the annual AWP (Association of Writers & Writing Programs) Conference and Split This Rock Poetry Festival, and have held workshops at universities, high schools, middle schools, and other poetry venues to spread the word regarding the mission of and the activism sparked by "Poets Responding to SB 1070."

One of the highlights was a press conference and symbolic Floricanto poetry and song rally held on Saturday, February 5, 2011, on the steps of the U.S. Capitol to bring attention to immigration issues under consideration by the Congress and other state governments that could directly affect the civil rights of all. We were also joined by veterans of the U.S. military, who brought attention to the plight of many vets being unjustly deported back to Mexico after having served in the U.S. Armed Forces, and by other poets who were attending the 2011 AWP Conference & Bookfair in Washington, DC.

The moderators have a combined history of more than forty years of nonviolent direct action campaign organizing experience between them, and they highlight other issues that fall under the rubric of poetry of resistance on their own Facebook pages. Poets who have served as moderators of our collective Facebook page are (in alphabetical order): Carmen Calatayud, Lorna Dee Cervantes, Antoniette Nora Claypoole, Iris De Anda, Elena Díaz Björkquist, Sharon Elliott, Sonia Gutiérrez, Israel Francisco Haros López, Andrea Hernández Holm, Scott Maurer, Edith Morris-Vásquez, Abel Salas, Raúl Sánchez, Hedy García Treviño, Alma Luz Villanueva, and Meg Withers. All of the moderators, past and present, continue to contribute to social justice campaigns, which include those addressing the issues of "Poets Responding." Another highlight of this work is our collaboration with Michael Sedano, the Tuesday editor of *La Bloga*, an online literary review that covers Chicana/o and Latina/o literature, news, and views. Along with Sedano, "Poets Responding to SB 1070" established a weekly online Floricanto in *La Bloga*, which features the selected works of poets who contribute to our page. This is a way not only to showcase the poets and their poems but also to widen the audience base for the issues raised by SB 1070 and xenophobia in general.

Along with *La Bloga* we have put out calls for poems on other poetry of resistance concerns. These cover a wide breadth of issues, stemming from the injustices happening in our world and the social movements that have arisen in the areas of class, race, domestic violence, war, world catastrophes, and the environment. Some of the special editions of the Floricanto have highlighted these occurrences:

- The June 2010 shooting of fifteen-year-old Sergio Hernandez Guereca, killed in Mexico by a U.S. Border Patrol agent.
- The January 2011 shooting of U.S. Representative Gabrielle Giffords and eighteen other people, who were gunned down during a constituent meeting in Arizona. Six people died, including federal District Court Chief Judge John Roll; Gabe Zimmerman, one of Representative Giffords's staffers; and a nine-year-old girl, Christina-Taylor Green.
- In March 2011, a special tribute to the people of Fukushima, Japan, hosted by Odilia Galván Rodríguez, which later became its own Facebook page, "Love and Prayers for Fukushima."
- The February 2012 fatal shooting of seventeen-year-old African American Trayvon Martin by a white neighborhood watch volunteer.
- In August 2012, a world reading protesting violence against women, in particular violence against the disappeared women of Ciudad Juárez, Mexico.

- In December 2012, the Sandy Hook Elementary School shooting in Newtown, Connecticut, in which twenty children and six adults were killed.
- In 2014, the wanton killing of unarmed Palestinian children and their families by Israeli forces in Gaza; the gunning down of African American Michael Brown in cold blood by a white police officer in Ferguson, Missouri; the deportation and deplorable treatment of women and children refugees fleeing the cartels and criminal elements in Central America; and, most recently, the killing of six and disappearance of forty-three college students from Ayotzinapa, Mexico.

This collection of poems represents a groundbreaking multicultural collective poetic project that involves thousands of engaged participants, hundreds of poems, and thousands of posted comments. The project has become a significant poetic outlet and open public forum for people of all ages and ethnic backgrounds, and it defines a new role for poetry and of poets in society in the digital age. This project also connects poetics and politics in the Latin American and Chicano/Latino tradition in which poets become the recognized voices of popular struggles facing common folk. We feel this is engaging and calls people to action.

We had to think about how to sift through all of the hundreds of poems we had received in order to come up with a representative collection of work to present to the University of Arizona Press. The editors decided that the poems to consider would be those that had been forwarded on to be featured in *La Bloga*. A process was devised whereby each poet-moderator received the poems and then voted on them. The votes were then tallied, and the poems that received the most votes were those the editors worked on to prepare the collection.

The end result is a unique multicultural anthology that is also multigenerational and geographically diverse. The volume includes poems in English and Spanish by emerging poets, as well as by such distinguished U.S. poets as Francisco Aragón, Devreaux Baker, Sarah Browning, Lorna Dee Cervantes, Susan Deer Cloud, Sharon Doubiago, Martín Espada, Juan Felipe Herrera, Genny Lim, Pam Uschuk, and Alma Luz Villanueva, among others. All have lent their support to this poetic call for national dialogue on healing, tolerance, reflection, and reconciliation.

Poetry of Resistance: Voices for Social Justice also serves as a poetic historical record of the aftermath of the passage of Arizona's anti-immigrant SB 1070, a law that targeted immigrants and encouraged racial profiling; the nation's subsequent copycat laws; and also the resulting humanitarian crisis of thousands of refugee children and their families fleeing violence, death, and the desperate conditions one finds in Central American countries in great distress.

Several themes run through this book of poems as a result of poets feeling compelled to respond to the issues facing immigrants:

- *Nature, roots, and land of ancestors*: Poems of ancestral ceremony, nature poems, poems about indigenous roots and myths.
- *Border, law, and terror*: Border poems, testimonials of fear, poems addressing the history of injustice and discrimination, bullying, and subjugation.
- *Against the New American Apartheid in all its forms*: Poems denouncing Arizona SB 1070, racial profiling, xenophobia, cultural misunderstandings, Arizona HB 2281 (which intended to do away with ethnic studies in Arizona), the new border wall, and the mistreatment of refugee children and their families fleeing Central American countries in distress.
- *Homages to family and fallen border crossers*: Family accounts, barrio poems, reaffirmations of shared identities, epic poems.
- *Resistance and solidarity*: Poems of resistance; calls for actions (like the ones advocating the Dream Act), such as demonstrations, marches, and protests; humorous poems.
- *Sacred spaces and new visions*: Sacred chants, poems of communal healing, calls for liberation, calls for comprehensive immigration reform.

In sum, this book is a work of the heart dedicated to the struggles of people trying to figure out where they belong on the basis of what their governments are doing and with whom they are collaborating. With the latest influx of child refugees from Central America, we know that the issue is bigger than first imagined, that it includes policies of the United States in Mexico and Central America, and that it involves the people trying to make their way in a world that has become larger than borders.

Francisco X. Alarcón
Odilia Galván Rodríguez
Editors

POETRY of RESISTANCE

PARA LOS NUEVE DEL CAPITOLIO

*Para los nueve estudiantes arrestados
en el Capitolio Estatal de Arizona por
protestar la ley SB 1070 el 20 de abril de 2010*

FRANCISCO X. ALARCÓN

carnalitos
y carnalitas
hermanos
y hermanas:

desde lejos
podemos oír
sus corazones latir

ellos son
los tambores
de la Tierra

nuestra gente
les sigue de cerca
sus pasos

como guerreros
de la justicia
y la paz

enfrentan
la Bestia
del odio

el uso
discriminatorio
de la policía

se encadenan
a las puertas del
capitolio estatal

para que el terror
no se escape hacia
nuestras calles

FOR THE CAPITOL NINE

*To the nine students arrested
at the Arizona State Capitol
protesting SB 1070 on April 20, 2010*

FRANCISCO X. ALARCÓN

*carnalitos
y carnalitas*
brothers
and sisters:

from afar
we can hear
your heartbeats

they are
the drums
of the Earth

our people
follow closely
your steps

as warriors
of justice
and peace

you take on
the Beast
of hatred

the unlawful
police enforcement
of discrimination

you chain yourselves
to the doors of
the State Capitol

so that terror
will not leak out
to our streets

sus voces
sus acciones
su valentía

no nos las pueden
ya arrebatar
ni encarcelar

ustedes son nueve
jóvenes guerreros
como nueve luceros

son la esperanza
los mejores sueños
de nuestra nación

sus rostros
son radiantes
como el Sol

y romperán
esta negra noche
para un nuevo día

sí, carnalitas
y carnalitos:
todos nuestros
hermanas y hermanos

no necesitan papeles
para probar
de una vez

"somos humanos
como ustedes son—
no somos criminales"

nuestra petición es:
"¡NO a la criminalización!
¡SÍ a la legalización!

your voices
your actions
your courage

can't be taken
away from us
and put in jail

you are nine
young warriors
like nine sky stars

you are the hope
the best dreams
of our nation

your faces
are radiant
as the Sun

they will break
this dark night
for a new day

yes, *carnalitas*
and *carnalitos*:
all our sisters
all our brothers

need no papers
to prove once
and for all

"we are humans
 just like you are—
we are not criminals"

our plea comes to:
"NO to criminalization!
YES to legalization!"

INVOCATION

*To the poets and all the people who in person or in spirit stood with
"Poets Responding to SB 1070" on the steps of the U.S. Capitol on
Saturday, February 5, 2011*

FRANCISCO X. ALARCÓN

we first form a circle
hands holding hands
warming each other

under a cold drizzle
wanting to turn Winter
into a Spring of Solidarity

a human Stonehenge
standing in front of
the U.S. Capitol in DC

we then call the North
the Land of our Ancestors
so we can have the Wisdom

with the deep roots
and the heights of Grandpa
and Grandma sequoia trees

we call forth the East
the Direction of Fire
where the Sun daily rises

so we can turn into living
torches giving out light
throughout the night

we also call the South
for the might of Water
to empower us here

and now to become rivers
carving canyons all the way
to the Sea of Freedom

we face and call the West
taking in this cold Wind
exhaling this warm Breath

forming a single cloud
that rises up as an offering
as a true Prayer of Unity

we come from the four
Directions of this Land
from plains, rain forests

from mountains, valleys
from deserts, towns
cities and nowhere

we are a dozen bards
rhyming in a single beat
springing from the heart

weaving with our voices
a tapestry, a waving banner
seeking Peace over War

we might be few, but
our Spirit is boundless
unbroken, and free

we are Moses speaking
to Pharaoh: "let our people
already here live in peace"

"stop the deportation
of veterans and bring
the deported home"

"for a humane comprehensive
immigration reform now
and civil rights for all"

may the deaf hear our plea
may the blind see our banners
may the classic columns dance

to the tune of tropical drums
of our new emancipation:
"aquí estamos y no nos vamos"

we are also sons and daughters
of this Land of the Brave and Free—
running buffaloes coming home

BORDERLESS COMPASSION

FRANCISCO X. ALARCÓN

what if you were *Chava*,
an eleven-year-old young boy
from the outskirts

of the capital city
of El Salvador, among
the poorest of the poor

your *Papá* whose own
father had been killed
on the street by the military

during the civil war
in the 1980s when he was
also only eleven years old

decides one day
to take off to *El Norte*
and promises you
and your *Mamá*
that he will send plenty
of dough that never arrives

forcing your *Mamá* to leave
in search for a better
life in California —

you weep at night
because you haven't seen
your *Mamá* in five years

she is becoming a ghost,
a fainting voice coming off
a neighbor's cell phone

she tells you not to come,
not to risk your own life
by joining the thousands

of children going North,
but the local *mara* gang
just killed your best friend

you're told you're next;
you have no option
but to call all family

relatives and friends
to lend you the money
for the journey North —

what if you were one
of the migrant kids arriving
from Central America

escaping this cruel cycle
of violence and death,
holding their lives

and their dreams
in their own small hands
willing to risk it all

wishing to join together
with their loving families,
becoming true refugees

migrant butterflies
trapped in a world in need
of borderless compassion

PORTIONS

JOANN ANGLIN

We eat from each other's plates
the tines of our forks clang in
the passing of morsels.

My spoon enters your mouth
your salt spills across my napkin
bad luck creeps over us both.

We don't have to exchange love to
know how we need each other—
we have cooked this situation together

me looking into your eyes, you looking
into mine. If we help each other, we
can avoid or heal scalds and cuts.

We can stir our pots together. We can
watch over each other's shoulders. We
can call out the warning.

POEM WITH A PHRASE OF ISHERWOOD

To Jan Brewer

FRANCISCO ARAGÓN

Cruelty is sensual and stirs you
Governor, your name echoing the sludge
beneath your cities' streets. It spurs

the pleasure you take
whenever your mouth nears
a mic, defending your law . . . your wall.

Cruelty is sensual and stirs you
Governor; we've noticed your face
its contortions and delicate sneer

times you're asked to cut
certain ribbons—visit a dusty place
you'd rather avoid, out of the heat.

Cruelty is sensual and stirs you
Governor, the vision of your state
something you treasure in secret

though we've caught a glimpse
in the jowls of your sheriff:
bulldog who doubles as your heart.

END OF AN AFFAIR

CATHY ARELLANO

Good-bye, United States.
It's clear you don't want me.
The mayor of Albuquerque proclaimed sanctuary
for ICE officials in the city's jails.
He gave *la migra* the right
to harass our sisters and brothers
off the streets
just as APD does
on the streets.

Farewell, U.S.
Arizona's cancer is spreading internally.
First, that sheriff plays like he's in a bad 1940s Hollywood movie
then he doesn't investigate more than 400 sex crimes
where the victims were brown
and dozens were children.
Today, twenty-one-year-olds can walk around Arizona
with a concealed and loaded weapon
without a permit
but students can't read books like *Occupied America*
'cuz America . . . isn't occupied?

I knew it was over back in Cali, Uncle Sam.
You wanna send my children
who've grown up here
to places they've never been
or are too young to remember.

I knew it was over years ago
when I found the numbers 187, 209
lining your pockets.
I was a fool to think I could change you.

But now, *¡Basta ya! ¡No más!*

I know you don't like it when I speak Mexican.
You studied in Spain
where their Spanish sounds like French or Italian
where they look French or Italian.

Sam, I'm tired of having a second-class accent in your ears
and a Third World body in your hands.

Come on, Sammy, no one can say we didn't try—
you tried to conquer me;
I tried to survive you.

Since it's over,
since we're done
through with each other
finally

I've spoken to my family
the ones who
tend the yards
clean the pools
deliver the mail
answer the phones
make the copies
move the furniture
drive the trucks
fix the cars
cash the checks that the banks won't

Just so you know,
Defender of the Free World,
my brothers told our cousins
who pick all that produce in the fields
slaughter the hogs and cattle
cook dishes from around the world
then wash them

And you know I talk to my sisters every day
They're waiting at their sewing machines,
computer terminals, and jumbo dryers

Our aunts and uncles are standing
by their vacuum cleaners
and shampooers on the office floors

My nieces and nephews have stopped asking,
"May I help you?
You want fries with that?"

Yes, they're waiting . . . for you.

This is our border
between our past and our future.
Our past where you invaded
and our future where you're evicted.

Don't worry, U.S.,
we won't make you swim home.
We don't hold you to the same standards
we hold for ourselves.

Our ship builders crafted a fleet
that will carry your funny hats
ruffled shirts
those black shoes with big brass buckles
all your guns
all your diseases
and you
back to where you came from.

Our *tortilleras* have neatly folded
"wrapped"
all your stuff into a huge tortilla
so you have a snack for your journey.

U.S., Uncle Sam,
look on the bright side,
they got democracy
and religious freedom
over there now.
The *two* things you came *here* for.

Consider yourself: Mission Accomplished!

What's that?

Radical
   Revolutionary
      Communist
        Socialist
          Crazy
            Outlaw

Savage

Queer
Me?

If those words mean I reject your
condemning my gods and goddesses
taking my land and water
kicking me out of school
throwing me in jail
locking up my books
telling me who I can or cannot love
controlling how many children I choose to have—if any
and all the rest of your
rules, regulations, and restrictions

Then, yes, all those words
you say about me are true.
And you're right—
I've never changed.

And God (mine—
you can have yours back)
only knows that
I've been praying for this day
since the first book banning
on my land—
when your cousin burned my codices.

So, Sam,
you found your way in,
you know the way out.
In case you forgot,
it's the door you kept trying to push me through.

I'm going to bed
to sleep,
to dream the sweetest dream,
Freedom.

NUESTROS NIÑOS Y NIÑAS

JORGE TETL ARGUETA

Nuestro niños y niñas
juegan con trocitos de madera
llevan mariposas en las manos
se levantan con los pájaros

Nuestros niños y niñas
cantan a la ronda
le hablan a las nubes
un día se van siguiendo sus sueños

Nuestros niños y niñas
vuelan
nadan
no le temen a La Bestia*

Nuestros niños y niñas
son guerreros
son gorriones
tienen vocales y coraje en sus corazones

Nuestros niños y niñas
no son extraterrestres o ilegales
son como los niños y niñas
de todo el mundo

Hermosos como el agua
como el viento
como el fuego
como el amanecer

---

*La Bestia: el tren que viaja a través de México a la frontera estadounidense.

OUR CHILDREN

JORGE TETL ARGUETA

Our children play
With small pieces of wood
They carry butterflies in their hands
They rise with the birds

Our children sing
Round and round
They speak to the clouds
One day they go following their dreams

Our children
Fly
Swim
They do not fear The Beast*

Our children
Are warriors
Are hummingbirds
They have voices and courage in their hearts

Our children
Are not aliens or illegal
They are like all children
Of the world

Beautiful like the water
Like the wind
Like the fire
Like the sunrise

---

*The Beast: the train that travels through Mexico to the U.S. border.

TATTOO SB 1070

ADRIÁN ARIAS

Adolorido el cuerpo se levanta
y descubre que el cielo no es firme
que las estrellas se mueven y no se caen
que los espejos son difíciles de atravesar
pero eventualmente los atraviesas y llegas
a ese lugar donde las estrellas
son agujeros en la piel de la noche
a ese lugar de fuegos artificiales
de alambre de púas y rayos de sol
que marcan tu cuerpo con el nuevo tatuaje
SB 1070

La noche con la que viajas de regreso a casa
es la más oscura y cierras los ojos
y descubres el cuerpo que se esconde en el cuerpo
en el borde invisible del tiempo
el ojo del cielo está vivo y dentro tuyo
el vestido de luz que es la piel del sueño
se transforma en tu propia carne
que lleva escrita la inscripción
SB 1070

Y te sacas la piel y la piel de tus hijos
y la piel de tu familia
y coses todas las pieles juntas
con la máquina de luz que es el miedo
quieres esconderlos en el vestido que es
la piel imposible de la libertad
y atrapada en las costuras
guarda mensajes de alivio, cartas de amor
fotos recortadas en forma de corazón
sobrecitos de azúcar
suvenires de una pesadilla en Technicolor
que llevan impresa la marca
SB 1070

oh cuerpo atrapado en la fabricación de sueños
cuando abras los ojos sólo vas a querer un
abrazo

abrazo
abrazo
pero sólo obtendrás
silencio
silencio
silencio
y una voz maquinal que a lo lejos te canta
SB 1070

LOOKING THROUGH CHAIN LINK AT MCALLEN STATION

For Edith

VÍCTOR ÁVILA

Although this young girl is not Ruby Bridges
and has never heard her name
she has the same heart of forgiveness
for those looking to blame
this anonymous child for every ill in the world
as she tries to get sleep in McAllen Station.

In her dreams she looks into the eyes of an ambiguous nation
and sees two completely different faces.
One speaks with empathetic eyes that understand her suffering.
While the other face . . . speaks about God's love and mercy
but, seemingly, only on Sundays.

She's awakened by the hum of fans on the ceiling—
beside her, a younger sister who is still sleeping.
She notices an orange butterfly just outside the window.
She wonders what it would be like to have wings
that could fly over any wall or any border.

No, her dreams of becoming a butterfly will not be denied.
Certainly not by those who shout venomous words
that she can't understand. She's beginning to learn
that forgiveness is greater than hatred found in some hearts.
And that humility is a sign of true strength no matter the circumstance.

It's as if God has polished her heart
and it now reflects his light for the world to see.
Her love is his love and a beacon for all
including those who protest her presence through ill-conceived notions.
Yes, the butterfly has flown and left McAllen Station
And flutters northward beyond the reach of ignorance and hatred.

LA REGLA DE LOS LADRONES

AVOTCJA

La Frontera
Grandísima fantasía
Laberinto malvado
Una monstruosidad increíble
Una mentira mortal
Hecho de alucinaciones santificadas
La Frontera
Una línea imaginaria
Nacida de la muerte y una dieta de miseria
Esta pesadilla venenosa
Fortificada de un montón de codicia
Solamente una soga moderna de hipocresía ilimitada
Una ilusión cruel
La Frontera
Un cuchitril lleno de bobería desmoralizada
Una casa grande creada de robo
Y nadando
En bañeras calientes de lágrimas importadas
La Frontera
Una línea pa' esconder un concepto artificial
Alrededor de vallas invisibles
Muros transparentes pa' proteger tierras robadas
La Frontera
Dos palabras endiabladas
Dos palabras malvadas
Dos palabras sucias
Reglas de
Ladrones bestiales que no tienen derecho de existir
En la tristeza indescriptible del corazón
De esta vieja poeta negra

THE LAW OF THIEVES

AVOTCJA

The Border
A bigger than life fantasy
An evil maze
An incredible monstrosity
A deadly lie
A creation of sanctified hallucinations
The Border
An imaginary line
Born of death and fed on misery
This poisonous nightmare
Armed and held up by a mountain of greed
Just a modern-day noose of unlimited hypocrisy
And cruel trickery
The Border
A hole full of soul-stealing stupidity
A mansion created by thievery
And swimming
In hot tubs of imported tears
The Border
Just a line hiding an artificial concept
Around invisible fences
Transparent walls to protect stolen lands
The Border
Two demonic words
Two evil words
Two filthy words
Laws of
Thieves and bullies that have no right to exist
In the too awful for words sadness in the heart
Of this old Black Poet

REASONABLE SUSPICION—THE CONQUEROR'S DREAM

DEVREAUX BAKER

He woke that morning
with the words in his mouth,
a bad taste he was used to.

He buckled his belt, pulled on his gun.
He rolled the words around his tongue.
He liked the bitter taste,

the copper aftertaste
that whispered his name
in a thousand reflections of the sun
off his badge.

He craved an adrenaline rush
to bring the words to life.
He drove through the streets
of his hometown
looking for someone
of reasonable suspicion.

They could be a woman,
singular, pregnant,
aging, or filled with the light
of future possibilities.

A child, a grandmother,
it did not matter
as long as they fit the
stereotype he had been handed.

He was on a mission
to find someone he could conquer,

as in a dream of suspicion
passed down from
past generations he claimed now

as his own.

He woke that morning
with the words in his mouth,
a bad taste he was used to.

LIGHTNING ON A BLACK NIGHT OVER THE CHUSKA MOUNTAINS

yaaishjaach'ili'.7.10

KRISTOPHER BARNEY

there's a part of me that becomes alive
becomes deadly aware of everything
in all the insane moments of my life
in every cloud shape
in the shapes of my homeland
in the faces
in the rough texture of brown bodies
where one can find
trails of beauty
parts of the eternal
passions ignited in the sensuality of the touch
that gives me goose bumps
the magic that happens
too sudden and less often and
yes i miss you and my mind
runs a separate road of longing of
absorbing beauty through silence and the
internal dialogue over the value of life and
words and actions given to
souls lost somewhere between
this world and the next
a dual battle between gods and men and the
gentle children who
walk in the first days of freedom
we still have it inside of us
this sense of freedom
everything before Columbus
before all the bullshit
this fragrance
this look in the eyes
in bodies tanned by desert winds
and blue sunned skies
beautiful brown bodies that
fit right into scenes of
red canyon bottomlands
brown eyes

black hair
the beauty that only Native can appreciate
this spirit that brings songs to me
in this early morning
all that i take in
when i'm on a journey
hell-bent on easing the lonesomeness and
momentary heartbreak of coming to terms with
this life
with seeing
the organs of the earth split open
the trembling nature of anger taking hold
when i walk through this land
see coal trains and trucks hauling
coal to power plants and hear the endless rhetoric
and debates of NDN politicians
hear the worthless discussions over
how life contains so little value next to pleasing
the greed of corporations and
the shadows that implode
as shareholders withhold their investments
as the world of Wall Street becomes
covered in seaside oil sludge
when all so-called transparency gets fogged
by the smokestacks of power plants and cities
the death
the black winds that cover us all and yet
all i can think of is you this morning
the restless night
the wrestling to sleep
this wind that surrounds me in the a.m. moment
the images fading through overcast and sun's
first light and the silent wishing to be
somewhere else
an escape from the torture of this life
the responsibility those like myself face
this road
this song
this act of pure resistance
this dance with eagle plumes and clouds
the lightning that strikes
through a black night over
the Chuskas . . .

SLAUGHTERS AND SHIFTS AND MIGRATIONS— ARIZONA

VIRGINIA BARRETT

I spent the day skirting the Mojave in nearly 100 degrees,
no air conditioning in the car, wondering how people can make it
in such heat, crossing the Sonoran Desert by foot to get to this side.

¡No expongas tu vida a los elementos! ¡No vale la pena!

Past nightfall I catch 66 through Seligman, wrecked and in need of a bed.
How do they sleep with pillows of cactus and scorpions under their heads?

I pull in after a neon motel sign: supai.
I receive the last available room from the affable owner.
She inquires about my profession, and her face brightens at my reply.
"When we first moved to America from India," she tells me,
"my son, he made the Taj Mahal from clay in school. He painted it, too.
Teaching art to children," she assures me, "this is very, very important."
She hands me my key with a sudden melancholy gesture.
"But in this small town," she shakes her head and glances outside,
"they have no art." She sighs, "So my children, they do sports
and computers instead."

My room, recently remodeled, is uninspiring but clean.
What can you expect for forty bucks?
But why am I complaining—an entire family could live in here
if they managed to make it over the border safely.
Los coyotes ahora cobran $4,000.

Supai—from *Havasupai*, the indigenous language of this land.
Slaughters and shifts and migrations;
greed and dreams and people searching to survive.

This morning, on the road again and already hot, grasshoppers perish
on my windshield as a bolt of lightning over the mountain I'm driving
toward
momentarily steals my eye.
The news says: "Some support the installation of a minefield
to keep illegal immigrants out." Arizona—how many need to die?

Moving over the land can push us into the heart of our existence,
beating and aching and keeping us alive.

What agony over killing these insects!
What exhilaration driving toward the rain
Earth holds the right to tell any of us where we belong.

LISTEN CHILD

For m'ijo

ESMERALDA BERNAL

listen child,
do not worry,
your red skin
has been the robe
of ancient wisdom.

what does your
teacher know
or does your teacher know
hate is her lecture.

do not cry,
wipe your tears
of many generations.
the universe
is your school.
let your teacher be
what she must be:
an example of
what not to be.

THE FLAG OF TOUCH

SARAH BROWNING

On the border with Mexico
we call it a fence, as if
to lean on its top, chat
with those neighbors
to the south, trade rakes,
trade gossip. Call it a fence,
call it a gate, call it good—
still, Nogales, Arizona,
Nogales, Sonora: trench,
ground sensors, infrared
night-vision scopes.

In Palestine, the land's already
been taken—families on one side,
orange groves on the other.
Ours is a culture of many walls
the Saudi poet writes
in her e-mail. Translated
into Japanese, her poems
vault the high barriers
of this world. Young people
sat on the Berlin Wall
and waved the flags
of their future.

I want a flag that waves
like that, for bricks
that go home in tourist
luggage, for the Saudi poet
and her sisters, for touch.
I want the flag of touch,
the flag of men waiting
for work in the morning
chill of the 7-Eleven parking lot,
the flag of nannies
pushing strollers to the park
for fellowship and swings,
flag of the women

who spend each day
changing the soiled sheets
of their new country.

I want the flag of talking,
of sitting on the disintegrating
wall and gabbing, gossiping,
negotiating, waving that flag
of no walls. That flag.

BORDER GHOST OF SONORA

CARMEN CALATAYUD

In this corner of the desert,
she has already died.
I pick up her broken mask,
promise to glue it together again.

My mother roams the border
she floats between the countries
she thought would share her heart.

My pillow saves the dreams
the dead have weaved,
banking on *milagros*.

I have a monsoon wish:
Let the rains wash away
the boots of the Border Patrol
so they step in flooded sand

because I am tired of *la migra*
who walk with feet of rock,
who clothe me in a cape of fear
who make me think
that God is a wolf in the night.

I string silver beads,
still believe in resurrections.
I get the phantom pains where the barbed wire
cut my mother's arms.

My hair has grown into a broom
it sweeps away the blisters,
drags along my washgun hope.

Café con leche keeps me awake
in case of visions *de mi mamá*.
She dreamed of dinnertime,
but I'm not hungry anymore.

I count moonbeam strips
and pray for shooting stars.
Listen for her whisper:
it sounds like purple silk.

AWAKENING AT NIGHT

*For "Poets Responding to SB 1070" and
Representative Gabrielle Giffords*

CARMEN CALATAYUD

Anger creeps
through my fingers
to tips that buzz
with frustration.
Marigolds pop
and wither,
turn into crust.

Under the gypsy moon
I witness my heart
of coal grow tentacles,
reach out to strangle
the pain my people hold.

Flamenco ancestors
play castanets,
express their rage
through the heels
of their shoes.

My stomach kicks
as Venus appears
in the red wing sky
and I feel the wise
child of belonging
who reminds me

That time has always
been on our side.

That our hands
protect the land
That our souls collide
moment to moment
That our sleep has been
disturbed for centuries
but we are never too tired
to speak the truth.

HOY MUJERES Y HOMBRES

XÁNATH CARAZA

Ciudad con campos de flores rojas
Donde cada pétalo lleva
El nombre de un estudiante que conocí

Hoy mujeres y hombres
Ya no niños inocentes
Ni adolescentes rebeldes
No hubo tiempo

Hoy mujeres y hombres que demandan justa causa
El derecho que no se debe de prohibir
Derecho a ser educados
A ser parte de la ciudad

En las ciudades
Donde los derechos
De igualdad no han nacido
Donde la voz de aquellos que atravesaron
La frontera sea tan válida como la de los demás
Las calles están vacías

Quiero recordar el color rojo
De los campos floridos
El reflejo del sol y del agua
La fuerza de sus palabras

Ya no hay niños inocentes
Ni adolescentes rebeldes
No hubo tiempo
Sólo mujeres y hombres forzados a crecer

TODAY WOMEN AND MEN

XÁNATH CARAZA

City with fields of red flowers
Where each petal carries
The name of a student I met

Today, women and men
No longer innocent children
Nor rebellious adolescents
There was no time

Today, women and men demanding a just cause
The right that must not be prohibited
The right to be educated
To be part of the city

In the cities
Where the rights
Of equality have not been born
Where the voices of those who crossed
The border be as valid as that of everyone else
The streets are empty

I want to remember the color red
Of the flowery fields
The reflection of the sun and the water
The strength of their words

No longer are there innocent children
Nor rebellious adolescents
There was no time
Only women and men forced to grow

ON THE BORDER, WE DREAM

For Rane Arroyo

HÉCTOR CARBAJAL

On the border, we dream about life
Because in the waking hours, there is death
We dream of roaming the earth
And we live and then die
And then grow again
And then die again—a cycle so sweet

On the border, I see the *viejitas* and *viejitos*
Walking through the downtown bus terminal
They walk as if they've traveled
Centuries through wind, rain, and thunderstorm
And then again—more travels for the weary

On the border, I dream about desire
Brown bodies resurrected from guilt
Brown bodies resurrected from blame
Brown bodies resurrected from violence
How many of us died before?
But we live again

On the border, you live again
Because your story died but
Someone else continues the end
To begin again—and again
These are the things we dream about
Only disrupted by the realities of waking hours

On the border we dream the beautiful
A soul consciousness collective
Imagine: A meditation that just is
A whirlwind to transport us
Elsewhere—

On the border, Rane, we remember you
A meditation upon who we are, who we were
What we become
And then reshift

You'll return to us
Again and again
To remind us to start over
again.

NIÑO TRAGA FUEGOS

ELIZABETH CAZESSÚS

Hola, señora:

Soy primitivo desde la raíz hasta la crisma,
lanza llamas, condenado al fuego,
condición de la miseria errante.

Soy limpia vidrios por la mañana
traga fuegos por la noche,
alquiler para pederastas
por la madrugada.

No necesita asomarse
al holocausto de Auschwitz
para saber lo que cuesta
una mirada

para hornos tengo este día
y vale lo que sea su voluntad.

OLMECAN EYES

LORNA DEE CERVANTES

Olmecan eyes gaze into the future,
a path of light piercing the forest,
heavy lidded with the past, ancient
sorrows carved into stone. With rain,
the present leaks into now, into the DNA
of fallen stars, the mystery of oceans,
the settled silt of settling into culture.

Olmecan eyes reborn. The infant
stone unfurling in our navels.
Another civilization reconquers
the wilderness of today. Sun devouring
Earth, we are shadows of the way
we were, beneath the shifting planets,
the comets, the desolate inconsolable moon.

Into the history of obsidian blades,
a human heart beats on the plate,
the slate of our division thinning
into someone's blood. The blood of
The People surging still beneath
the pursed lips, the pierced tongue,
the sudden pulse. We are The People

still. Our constitution stolen
from us in the fear. We rise, not
vengeful, but full of the peace
of knowing, our present tense.

DEL PUENTE AL ARCO

ANA CHIG

Nubes imponen el silencio en los hostales
Lejanas sombras se congregan al calor de neumática
fogata
Una manta de liquen y el sopor del invierno ovilla
mi cuerpo—junto a ellos—

Todo es posible en el asidero fantasioso de la urbe
Hombres y quimeras residen en los rincones,
bajo el puente
Afiladas puntas penetran sus venas, un río negro
les circula nutrida la esperanza

En acodo, deletreo lejanos muros que contienen más
            sangre que razones
Un cúmulo arriscado sobresale tras los techos
junto al arco
El campaneo parroquial—y su ausencia—induce obligada,
            la partida.

RECONSIDER THE LILIES

JABEZ W. CHURCHILL

The dark,
night's starry crown,
does not flee the floodlights
but reigns beyond our sight
on both sides of the border.
Nor does the oak
outside the bathroom stir
while I lie awake
in expectation of the dawn,
but drinks more deeply from the earth below.
Nor do the cats lose sleep,
unequal to the dawn.
But still, I wonder
if I shall ever see
wall and wire recycled,
five hundred miles of taquerias and ice cream stands
open front and back,
and anxious fear
that most will be asleep
at opening time.

CONSIDERAD DE NUEVO LAS AZUCENAS

JABEZ W. CHURCHILL

La noche,
su corona estrellada,
no huye de los faroles
sino reina
más allá de nuestra vista
por ambos lados de la frontera.
Ni tiembla el roble
encima de la bañera
donde inquieto me acuesto
esperando el alba
sino bebe más profundo de la tierra.
Ni los gatos
pierden sueño,
desiguales al amanecer.
Pero sigo inseguro
si llegare a ver
pared y alambre reciclados,
quinientas millas de taquerías y heladerías sirviendo ambos
lados,
y ansioso temo
que todos seguirán durmiendo
a la hora de comenzar.

THE NEW WEST

ANTOINETTE NORA CLAYPOOLE

1.

an ancient trade route tells of toads
in the autumn desert sonora scaling
skies. toads leap defying time. a legend.
like Billy the Kid and his perplexing pardon.
Pat Garrett and his murder of the west. kiva
maps kiva secrets kiva stone people ladder
inward like that diamond in a heart old poets
define a remedy a random act of majestic.
amulet. purple saged toad seekers sleep deep
sweet baby the police will take all you dare dream.

2.

he drives down the old highway like Morrison in "American Prayer."
seeking autumn toad lore snazzy miami vice DEA agents
surround sound the desert. dark. orwellian vehicles
clandestine seizures. old powder blue. mercedes. searched. puppy
eyes desperado *no habla español*. toads, officer.
drug road kid. drug cartels use this highway
kid. seriously? hunting toads? not a Tom Robbins
frog legs in pajamas piece. more tasered space more DEA
more unmarked cars. two hours crimson King twilight. no drugs
no connections all alone with Spartacus Orthea the huntress
the pie-eyed pooch from Washington State who chews willow.
smiling through the rhetoric of philosophy the young man muse recites.

3.

the u.s. government hunts brownskinned young men
on sonoran desert highways like Garrett and Geronimo
a postcolonial cactused war two-lane road Marshalls are
like sideways 1950s Jesuit monks, exotic butterfly collectors.
pinning wings to placards. they are. bored. and twisted spectators.
captured in the capture fossilized in the kill, stainless stolen pins
sealing freedom under glass. sassing back into winged extinction.
soon the fires soon the scorch of torch that lights a yesterday.
and a generation of toads search sci-fi helicopter overflights
looking for a rare, human sighting to tell them kiva stories to the Sky.

SONNET FOR POLICE OFFICERS CHARGED WITH ENFORCING SB 1070

KAREN S. CÓRDOVA

I ask each Arizona officer,
respectfully, when you identify
illegal immigrants, please remember:
more than 100,000 Irish eyes
are lawlessly smiling on U.S. soil;
racist code for "without papers" is WOP;
your ancestors were strangers here — their toil
seeded your freedom. Bullies kick kids. Stop
striking *la gente*, who only see hope,
when they risk their lives to clean stained toilets,
maybe yours. Arrest thieves, terrorists, dope
dealers of all shades. Protect us from threats
to Señora Liberty: *pendejos*
and their white bigot fence 'round Chicanos.

TO BE A POCHA OR NOT TO BE

IRIS DE ANDA

because I'm neither
from here or there
I speak both languages
with a flair
born in Los Angeles
with roots that extend
reaching out to faraway lands
faraway sands, far away from here

because I'm my father's daughter
drowning in alcohol
seeking the metaphysical
calling back in time
my family line
a forgotten leaf
on the familia's tree
to be a *pocha* or not to be

because I'm my mother's daughter
drowning in depression
seeking a connection
recovering memories
of a tierra I never knew
a forgotten trace
of ancestors in me
to be a *pocha* or not to be

because I'm not good enough
for here or there
I love to hate my flag and
hate to love my creation
ashamed of Spanish in the first grade
I'm sorry Mami I never meant to hurt you
ashamed of English in *abuela*'s embrace
I know you never meant to hurt me

because I'm merging *culturas*
every time I breathe
crossing borders

every time I speak
split forever into one
at the edge of two worlds
the edge of possibility
to be a *pocha* or not to be

because I'm finding a balance
of this cosmic *raza*
a fusion of color
for this mestiza
things to learn
and things to teach
the little ones in front of me
to be a *pocha* or not to be

CAPITOL POETRY

on the cold winter steps of the U.S. Capitol, Washington, DC,
Saturday, February 5, 2011

NEPHTALÍ DE LEÓN

it was bitter cold
old snow was on the ground
from many places poets came
each with a brave bold heart

Tlaloc's tempered rain
came down to bless
each poet on the list
from time to time
Ehecátl, the wind,
softened his winter blast
millions of relatives
joined them there
the many back home
and spirits of the past

ghosts danced
each word gave truth
to their power voice
word arrows hit their mark
on the steps of the capitol stones

unequivocal voices rose
a native hymn to the parent sky
and there before the world
amerindian verses spoke
stop the genocide stop the raids

truthfully they but no bitter heart
spoke for the folks back home
we won't be silent by the side
we'll fight and resist as we always have
as long as Tlaloc has rain and mist
as long as the wind blows we'll insist
we're home, you can remain
we'll talk about your illegal claim
and keep you warm in the cold cold rain!

YOUR AMERICA, MY TURTLE ISLAND

SUSAN DEER CLOUD

In your America, you watch CNN for hours,
eat junk food, cheer your cowboy president
when he brags about invading Iraq.
In my Turtle Island, I watch polluted sky
through South Side window, imagine
what Binghamton was like before the white man
invaded these hills, this river valley.

In your America, your flags sprout
on your porches like dyed carnations . . .
red, white, blue in a forced spring.
In my Turtle Island, I grow flowers
in small pots filled with the earth
your America stole from us.

In your America, no one dies when you bomb
human beings in another country.
They just get liberated.
In my Turtle Island, I grow a red geranium
for my mother who died of *your* cancer . . .
a white gardenia for my father who died
for *your* freedom in your "Good War" . . .
a blue violet for the sky of my heart.

In your America, you make believe
that everyone lives in a nuclear family,
instead of the nuclear fission of dysfunction.
In my Turtle Island, I'm a mixed-blood Indian woman
who loves a Korean American poet
with a full blood's eyes and hair . . . and
a Persian cat, our daughter, color
of Iraqi sands.

In your America, you shout "Democracy,"
even though money is king and brings
your God into it. The one I don't trust.
In my Turtle Island, I speak my vision with what
Haudenosaunee people call "the Peacemaker's voice."
I only need enough fried bread to live on . . .
and silence for the Great Mystery.

In your America, you support Homeland Security,
confident no soldier or policeman will ever force you
onto a Trail of Tears, no lawyer, no trial.
In my Turtle Island, people are too poor to buy
their way out of reservations, cockroach slums,
jail archipelagos. I know what it's like
to be invaded by *your* freedom.

In your America,
will you ever know how it feels to love
a family, a tribe, this sweet bitter beautiful country,
my broken home . . .
the way I have loved
my Turtle Island for centuries?

BEFORE THE WORLD WAKES

ELENA DÍAZ BJÖRKQUIST

In the stillness of early morning
before the pale rays of dawn
hearken the first glorious glow,
Mother Nature is in a state of flux,
her energy stable.

Free of disordered vibrations,
my mind remains in the land
of slumber, although awake.
Deep sleep washed away impurities
accumulated from yesterday.

My mental, physical, emotional potential
is heightened to meditate in this peaceful,
energetically charged in-between time.
I connect in intimate fashion
with the Divine.

Light, air, energy flow around me,
speak in hushed tones of the day to come,
set my mood for a serene, fulfilling day.
In the glorious glow of morning
I wake as the world awakes.

Embracing the joy of being,
I draw upon the unique energy of
daybreak for comfort, creativity, vigor.
I feel blessed with the gift of
another day of life.

The sun's ascension inspires me, as it
grows golden to the birds' serenade.
My vitality returns as I become
one with the stirring of other beings
rubbing sleep from their eyes.

I greet the sun, the new day
in the traditional ancient way,
like my grandmother before me,
and her mother before her.
I call out in the four directions.

First to the north, *tahui, tahui,*
tahui, tahui.
Then to the east, *tahui, tahui,*
tahui, tahui,
To the south, *tahui, tahui,*
tahui, tahui,
and to the west, *tahui, tahui,*
tahui, tahui.

I return to the center,
open my arms, embrace the world.
I am centered, my destiny
not yet written,
there is nothing I cannot do.

TWO MISSING MEN, ONE WHITE, ONE BROWN, ONE RICH, ONE NOT SO RICH

ELENA DÍAZ BJÖRKQUIST

I hear a helicopter flying low,
rotors thump-thumping
as it crisscrosses the foothills.
I hear people calling a man's name
while they search the washes.
I read about it in the newspaper
Tanque Verde man missing,
Goes for a walk, doesn't come home.
Neighbors fear the worst.
I hear a TV newscaster
repeat the story.
The search continues for five days.

I remember another missing man.
Several years ago, Nico,
my niece Tina's partner
went for a walk and
didn't come home.
She reported him missing to the police.
No helicopters thump-thumping
in their Flowing Wells neighborhood.
No people searching the washes,
No story in newspapers or TV.
Instead, Tina questioned by police.
Did they fight? Why would he leave?
They asked her neighbors
the same insinuating questions.

Tina trudged to work every day,
cuddled her son, caressed her growing
belly, felt life begin to move.
Only after she put Nicolás to bed
did she allow feelings to surface.
Buried her face in Nico's clothes,
smelled the last shirt he'd worn,
his scent growing fainter day by day.
Clutched his wallet, money

and driver's license tucked inside.
Told herself, *he didn't abandon me.*
In bed, she fingered his Marine
dog tags like a rosary,
prayed he was safe.
Tears dampened her pillow.

A year later, Nico's mother
brought his dental records,
took them to the coroner's office.
They matched those
of a *Hispanic male*, found
two blocks from Tina's house
the day Nico went missing.
Notations read: *No ID.*
New running shoes.
Probably illegal.
DOA of a heart attack.

She learned Nico was buried
in potter's field, a "Juan Doe'"
the very same day
his son Giovani was born.
The women had Nico's body
disinterred, cremated,
chose an urn, gave him
a proper funeral for family
and friends to say good-bye.

Two missing men,
one white,
one brown,
one rich,
one not so rich.
Both found in Tucson.

THERE IS A FENCE AROUND MY HEART

JAMES DOWNS

There is a fence around
My heart and if I do not
Tear it down it will
Dismantle me I can see
The others on the other
Side waiting waiting for
Me to let them in and
If I don't I will be alone
With my rabid thoughts
There is a fence around
My heart and if I do not
Tear it down it will
Dismantle me

A CEREMONY FOR RECLAIMING LANGUAGE

especially for Casie Cobos and Gabriela Ríos

QWO-LI DRISKILL

our homelands remember us
they raise themselves up
to mend our tongues
remove fingers of conquistadors and
governors from bruised necks

as you enter
into this ceremony
breathe phrases
like copal smoke
let syllables strengthen
your blood like nopales
wear words
around your throat
a gift of turquoise and gold

remember
we are here to become elders
and ancestors who teach
our children to
heal the world

as you enter into this ceremony
say a prayer
offer tobacco
remember each morning
we enter into spinning
light of a galaxy that
loves us

hidden words will sprout
in your dreams
like *maíz* opening
into the rich brown soil
of Anáhuac

as your enter into this ceremony
mourn for what was stolen
smuggle your tongue
across their imaginary border
and laugh
let this language suture
your heart

each word whispers
a story
through your lips
weaves a basket
that carries
a mending
world

BORDER

SHARON DOUBIAGO

1.
Border
our mother is looking out our picture window with her binoculars
tracking the dark men
trekking across the blue mountains, our
southern horizon. Our
million-dollar Ramona view. Our

illegal workers our father has hired. This has always been
illegal, the smudge pots in the avocado and orange groves
burning cold nights throughout
the Santa Maria Valley

and the boys of my class
are sneaking the other way
across the border
to get to the girls for sale
in the Tijuana whorehouses

so beside themselves, so swollen
with merciless lust, we must allow them
this relief. Girls can't imagine
such pain though our fathers
ache in remembrance

in this end of America, cornered
all sides, the East and North our families are in exile from, the
West the unfathomable ocean, and the South

the Border. South of which is
nothing. Nothing
always there in our picture window, the blue
turning purple mountains a vast
unknowable inhuman Ocean

"Mexican" like the *n* word. The dark people
are trying to get here, we are not
trying to get there

except for the boys and the fathers
to the houses of prostitution

inside our house, inside our view, an armed border inside
the family

2.
our mother is sneaking food and water to them hiding in the rocks
past our father, she is telling me this, as if a question, as if to answer
a question, as if she knows I've gone beyond
the border of her understanding

like the wives who hid the Natives
in their closets and food storages
while their husbands hunted them down
on command of the California governor
in 1852

always adding, piercing me with her eyes
the legal ramifications
if we are caught, what would happen, but
the good we are doing by breaking the law, the bravery it takes, our
integrity and compassion, and always the savings so necessary
always the savings so admirable

and then always her indignant "but only English in the schools!"
To me getting my master's in English.
"English: the one and only official language."

Oh, Mama, that's your beloved grandmother
washing your mouth out with soap

your Indian grandfathers moonshining
to feed you

your brain of two realities, Mama
imagine the brain with no borders, every language
a different soul, imagine all the many other worlds united
as in the beginning, Mama

3.
And your mother, Ramon, your unknown Nothing
Kumeyaay Mesa Grande

mother is disappearing
Tijuana, August, 1955, the year
you are told
who you are, ward
of the court

your mother
walking with friends
down from San Diego
arm and arm up Revolución

when two men grab her from behind, pull her
into the alley

men full of lust, merciless nature
perhaps too poor to buy
a body worker

the last she is ever seen, your

border your
mother your family
you will never be able to cross
"she disappeared with the Mexicans,"
you sneer and sneer, then disappear
into Vietnam

through you are "Mexican" too
though you could not know this
Mexico
when California was Nothing
and for 1200 years before that, your

ancestral graves
both sides
the International Border
through the heart
of the Kumeyaay nation

from fifty miles south down Baja
to fifty miles north up Cupa
from the Colorado to the Ocean
a whole nation

and Cupa, the international
crossroads capital, a great city
of the world

4.
I am listening to the sprinklers going on
in my sister's Solano Beach condominium, the illegals
beneath my guest bedroom window
gardening in the dark
so as not to be seen
whispering in Spanish, *p'lapaneco*

Healer, she has to charge a lot
for her body work, she is explaining again
to afford this magnificent place

and our mother with her binoculars is looking out the back window
of their RV in Oaxaca. She is telling me this again and again
as if trying to say something
about the "Indian girl with the baby on her back"
climbing the rocks. Who is turning

and looking back at her
through the tinted glass. "She knew
I was watching her. She knew
exactly where to look. She looked
directly into my eyes, though she could not
have seen me. She looked at me
with hate. That was when I knew
this was her home. And so strange, she looked like
Chelli." My brother's daughter, her
granddaughter

5.
I finally say okay. My sister has me lie down
on the cement flower slab outside
I heard them working on last night. She is working
on me,
the tightly secured border
of our family

the whispering *tlapaneco*
your mother so long dead, Ramon

you are Vietnamese
missing in action

and Tecate
is Ramona's sister city now

and on Mesa Grande

your Coyote brothers
are setting off for work

"Geez!" she exclaims. "You should be dead!
I've never worked on anyone
who had all their points dead."

Our family reinforcing the burning smudge pots
of my soul

What's on the other side?
Cross it

BORDER CROSSING

SHARON ELLIOTT

A umba wa ori
A umba wa ori
Awa osun
Awa oma
Leri oma
Liki awo
Ara Orun
Ka a we˚

I am going back before the funeral
the crossing brings me to the land of my ancestors
before the singing starts
the banshee wails
the pipers float their cries upon the wind

I look at all the borders
crossed or left alone

who is dragged there
who comes willingly
who is ready
who is not

I have been here all my life
standing at the invisible line
between being
and not being
between this world and the next

next
next door
neighbors

as I prepare to cross
I know that it won't be a crossing
it will be an acceptance
flowing

˚Traditional Lucumi (African Cuban) chant to call the ancestors.

flowering
embracing

ten thousand feet
have walked this path
been thrown across that line
that lie

few chose it
their homes reduced to rubble and smoke behind their backs
their farmer's hearts
forced to the sea
to sit on rocky wasted land
or on the boulders of the shore itself
forced to exchange their meat and wool and milk
for unfamiliar fish
that don't come easily, if at all
to nets cast by untutored hands

weeping accompanies their journey
out of the green and fertile highland valleys
into the lairs of other clans
tribal people who will not yield easily
until they too are forced to join the march

and what new border can they visualize
how can they keep each other straight
they learn to pull their plaid garments
up around their shoulders
over their heads
the threads and colors creating small visual borders on the cloth
screaming THIS IS ME!
my identity
my land
the place I long to lay down to rest
I carry it with me in sacred cloth

and when I am ready
when I have reached the road's ending
and the last border stands before my feet

I will cleanse and wrap my body myself
before the ministrations of loving hands can do it for me

and I will go back
I will be back
I will smell the peat and heather
I will hear the birds and pipes
The laurel tree and hazel hedge will welcome me

the voices that I hear shall speak all the languages I have
gathered
and sing to me in one I do not know
but carry always in my heart

LA VOZ DEL INMIGRANTE

MARIO ÁNGEL ESCOBAR

Yo soy la espina dorsal
El canto al final del día
El que acaricia
la voluptuosa tierra
Ella y yo somos uno
Las manos que arrancan
y recogen
el fruto
para satisfacer
tu hambre
Yo soy el tierno callo
el viento desnudo
la nueva lengua
la sangre buscando paz
Yo soy el labio silente
y la mirada que grita

IMMIGRANT VOICES

MARIO ÁNGEL ESCOBAR

I am the backbone
An equal to any
The chant at the end
of the day
I am the caresser
of voluptuous earth
She and I become one
The hands that pluck and pick
to satisfy your hunger
I am the tender callus
the naked wind
the new tongue
flesh seeking peace
I am the silent lip
the gaze that shouts

ISABEL'S CORRIDO

Para Isabel

MARTÍN ESPADA

Francisca said: Marry my sister so she can stay in the country.
I had nothing else to do. I was twenty-three and always cold, skidding
in cigarette-coupon boots from lamppost to lamppost through January
in Wisconsin. Francisca and Isabel washed bedsheets at the hotel,
sweating in the humidity of the laundry room, conspiring in Spanish.

I met her the next day. Isabel was nineteen, from a village where the elders
spoke the language of the Aztecs. She would smile whenever the ice pellets
of English clattered around her head. When the justice of the peace said
You may kiss the bride, our lips brushed for the first and only time.
The borrowed ring was too small, jammed into my knuckle.
There were snapshots of the wedding and champagne in plastic cups.

Francisca said: The snapshots will be proof for Immigration.
We heard rumors of the interview: they would ask me the color
of her underwear. They would ask her who rode on top.
We invented answers and rehearsed our lines. We flipped through
Immigration forms at the kitchen table the way other couples
shuffled cards for gin rummy. After every hand, I'd deal again.

Isabel would say: *Quiero ver las fotos.* She wanted to see the pictures
of a wedding that happened but did not happen, her face inexplicably
happy, me hoisting a green bottle, dizzy after half a cup of champagne.

Francisca said: *She can sing corridos*, songs of love and revolution
from the land of Zapata. All night Isabel sang corridos in a barroom
where no one understood a word. I was the bouncer and her husband,
so I hushed the squabbling drunks, who blinked like tortoises in the sun.

Her boyfriend and his beer cans never understood why she married me.
Once he kicked the front door down, and the blast shook the house
as if a hand grenade detonated in the hallway. When the cops arrived,
I was the translator, watching the sergeant watching her, the inscrutable
squaw from every Western he had ever seen, bare feet and long black hair.

We lived behind a broken door. We lived in a city hidden from the city.
When her headaches began, no one called a doctor. When she disappeared

for days, no one called the police. When we rehearsed the questions
for Immigration, Isabel would squint and smile. *Quiero ver las fotos,*
she would say. The interview was canceled, like a play on opening night
shut down when the actors are too drunk to take the stage. After she left,
I found her crayon drawing of a bluebird tacked to the bedroom wall.

I left too and did not think of Isabel again until the night Francisca called
to say:
Your wife is dead. Something was growing in her brain. I imagined my wife
who was not my wife, who never slept beside me, sleeping in the ground,
wondered if my name was carved into the cross above her head, no epitaph
and no corrido, another ghost in a riot of ghosts evaporating from the skin
of dead Mexicans who staggered for days without water through the desert.

Thirty years ago, a girl from the land of Zapata kissed me once
on the lips and died with my name nailed to hers like a broken door.
I kept a snapshot of the wedding; yesterday it washed ashore on my desk.

There was a conspiracy to commit a crime. This is my confession: I'd do it
again.

GIVING VOICE

Dedicated to La Bloga *and all "Poets Responding to SB 1070"*

ODILIA GALVÁN RODRÍGUEZ

no choice
but to speak out—
loud about injustice
those who must hide have no voice, just
slashed tongues

they hide
while being used
by people who speak lies.
they work, live silently in fear
waiting

who then
will speak for us
when others turn away
who joins in solidarity—
speaks up

unearths
muted voices
teaches them new songs to sing
dedicates them poems for peace—
flowers

flor y canto
poder—[power]
sweet medicine to heal
fear, hatred and, yes, to demand
justice

BORDER INQUEST BLUES

ODILIA GALVÁN RODRÍGUEZ

at what crossing
could my poems
become bread
or water to offer
a people
the thousands
who cross so many
miles of misery

perched on trains
like birds
with clipped wings
who only fly
in their dreams
but decide to search out
the promise of a better life
at any cost

which of my
careful word choices
make a difference
to scorched tongues
that can no longer
even form a whisper
let alone cry out for help
in a desolate desert

there are no
flights on 747s
for a people
with only prayers
without papers
thick with words
that legitimize them
in an illegal world

full of legalized criminals
who form tempests
to tease out fear, and who

year after year
think up new ways to hate
at the same time take
even a person's last breath
if it benefits their profits

at what checkpoint
do my words become
more than arrows
sharp in their bite
or mere criticisms of the "Right"
still not hitting the target
or putting an end
to this war

COLLECTING THOUGHTS FROM THE UNIVERSE

ODILIA GALVÁN RODRÍGUEZ

What do the stars say
about children dying
or is it their spirits
twinkling down
big smiles on their faces
there's no suffering there
At the border
people act less than human
frighten traumatized children
in yellow school buses
their small faces pressed
against the windows
They see
the gnashing teeth
hear shouts of rage
What kind of war
is being waged here
these children fleeing war
fleeing death
looking for a place to dream
or looking for what's left
of their family
that's already flown away
for fear or promise
We wage wars
support criminal
heads of state
murderous coups
genocide
The false war on drugs kind
the raining down bombs
on innocents kind
the scaring of innocent children
riding on yellow school buses kind
the murdering of unarmed black people kind
And whom do we help
does all this war make life better
who is the real enemy
in a land

where one percent of people
owns more wealth
than the rest of us put together and
can we be put together again?

IMMIGRANT CROSSING

DANIEL GARCÍA ORDAZ

My father's feet
Carried the sesquicentennial stench of
Mexico, turned Texas, turned United States of America.

He labored in twenty-four- and forty-eight-hour shifts
Irrigating arid citrus groves,
Working under the bellies of navel orchards
In trenches that emanated a stink
That America could not stomach.

Mother Nature painted on my father's immigrant feet
Socks of earth, wind, and fire,
Then drowned them in her melting pot,

Ankles aching,
Bunions burning,
Blisters bleeding,
Calluses calcifying,
Nails embedded with myriad funguses
Frolicking frivolously
Only to become penitent parasites.

My father left
Mexticacán, Jalisco—
Less than a speck
On the Mexican map—
And crossed the Río Grande
For the privilege of standing on American soil,
For the privilege of owning an American acre,
For the privilege of raising his American children,
For the privilege of ruling
Over endless, waveless American ditches.
For the privilege of working
For endless, thankless sonofabitches.

On toasty Texas summer nights
When he'd come home at dawn,
We knew he was home upon smell,
As he shed his black boots

With a sigh of repose,
Crossing his feet
Under Uncle Sam's nose.

THE ONES WHO LIVE ON

NANCY AIDÉ GONZÁLEZ

I come from a long line of Mexican women
who washed their clothes on washboards in a bucket,
who worked in the fields,
who worked as maids in wealthy households,
who made tortillas at dawn
and boiled beans at dusk,
fed the chickens in their backyards,
watered their lush green plants,
disciplined their children,
and rarely questioned their husbands.

These women fought to survive
swallowed their tears
hid their fears.
My foremothers never gave up;
even when times were difficult they took
hardship with dignity.

My great-grandmother and grandmothers
were women who went to church
and prayed
had faith
and believed in God.
They were excellent mothers and wives,
the cornerstones of the family.

My mother was strong
when her husband cheated on her,
beat her,
verbally abused her,
then left her with two children
standing by his closed casket.

My aunt was wild,
adventurous, hilarious,
fun loving,
and abandoned by her only love
with a child to care for all alone.

These women were survivors
whose blood runs through my veins.

Yes,
I come from a long line of women
tough as nails,
hard as steel,
soft like velvet,
exquisite,
sweet like pan dulce,
full of wisdom,
stories,
secrets that will never be told.

They are my past,
they are my present,
they are my future.

They live in my heart,
these women with lyrical voices,
they are what brings me to keep walking
when all I want to do is go into a deep dark sleep
and never wake up.
They keep me alive when
I feel too weary to go on.

They are the force
that reaches out to touch my soul,
they are the hands that lift me up when I have failed,
they bathe me when I am covered in mud.

They are my foremothers,
they are the past,
they are the present,
they are the future,
they are the ones who live on.

LA VIRGEN DE LAS CALLES

For Esther Hernández

NANCY AIDÉ GONZÁLEZ

She stands on the
busy street corner
selling delicate red
and white roses
hugged by baby's breath
and luminous cellophane
resting in a
once discarded
plastic bucket.

She understands the innate
beauty of roses,
their fragility
their fragrant hope
as they grow slowly
from bud to emerge
embracing change
as they flush into
full bloom.

She knows of
piercing thorns
and truth of crossing
barbed wire borders.

She understands
the prickling sting,
the aculeus
of being an outsider.

She wears a large
sweatshirt with USA
emblazoned in block
print across her chest
but she misses Mexico
and the small town
she was raised in.

A red and green
rebozo hangs down
upon her head, shielding
her from the fulgent sun,
a gift from her mother,
a reminder of home.

People stride past her
lost in their own thoughts,
hustling to work,
on pressing errands,
wandering down the tangle
of the Los Angeles landscape.

She is La Virgen de las Calles,
waiting with a
heavy heart,
full of yearning,
dreaming of
new horizons,
a fountain of
humble tenderness
and abounding love.

La Virgen de las Calles
comprehends the
nature of roses,
their vulnerability,
their need for nettle.

MI BANDERA

SONIA GUTIÉRREZ

Mi bandera es del color de la flora—
de amarillos, verdes crespos y secos,
y de rosados encendidos: son las caritas
de flores y botones por sonreír.

Mi bandera es del color de la fauna—
de matices cremosos y oscuros
y de un pecho azul verde resplandeciente:
es el galope inquieto levantando el polvo y el grito
desgarrador emplumado.

Mi bandera es del color del agua—transparente
arropándome con sus brazos sin pugnar por el color
de la piel: en ella—río, gozo, canto, lloro y vuelvo
a sentirme amada.

Mi bandera no es del color de un arroyo rojo
de la sangre derramada de mi hermano palestino,
de mi hermana africana, de mi hermano blanco,
de mi hermana china y de mi hermano sediento.
mi bandera es el vaivén de una mano y un pañuelo
como un pájaro mensajero dolido buscando un monte
de esperanza ofreciendo paz y libertad.

MY FLAG

SONIA GUTIÉRREZ

My flag is the color of flora—
of yellows, crisp and dry greens,
and of bright pinks: they are the little faces
of flowers and buds to soon smile.

My flag is the color of fauna—
of creamy and dark hues
and of a radiant greenish-blue chest:
it is the restless gallop stirring dust and the feathered
heartrending scream.

My flag is the color of water—clear
embracing me with its arms without fighting over skin
color: in it—I laugh, I rejoice, I sing, I cry, and I feel
loved again.

My flag is not the color of a red stream
of spilled blood from my Palestinian brother,
from my African sister, from my white brother,
from my Chinese sister, and from my thirsty brother:
my flag is the swaying of a hand and handkerchief
like a wounded messenger bird searching for a mount
of hope offering peace and liberty.

GRANDCHILDREN OF THE UNITED FRUIT COMPANY

For Claudia González

SONIA GUTIÉRREZ

Knock, knock, knock.
America, there are children
knocking at your door.
Can you hear their soft
knocks, like conch
shells whispering
in your ears?

Weep, weep, weep.
Can you hear
the children whimpering?
Their moist eyes
yearning to see friendly TV-gringo houses
swing their front doors
wide open.

America, America, America!
The children are here;
they have arrived
to your Promised Land,
sprinkled with pixie dust,
paved with happiness
and freedom.

America, why do these children
overflow your limbo rooms?
Why are the children corralled
in chain link fences,
sleeping on floors
and benches?

America, did you forget
your ties dressed in camouflage
and suits in that place
called the Banana Republic?

What say you, America?
Please speak. And speak
loud and clear—
so the brown pilgrim
children never forget
the doings
of your forked tongue
and their color schemed
prison's-eye view.

CERRANDO HERIDA

ISRAEL FRANCISCO HAROS LÓPEZ

between the border songs
between the *rancheras* and corridos
bouncing off the walls of arizona
juárez tejas east los y minnesota
between the drumming and screeches
the handcuffs and paper trails

between the river from the *herida abierta*
the wound starts to close over and over
with every poem with every essay
with every palpable and unswallowable word

a holocaust disseminates
between the sounds of don't use that word
unless we're speaking of a jewish genocide
i say always remember a native holocaust
that hitler remembered and reconstructed
to create his nation

between citizen's arrest and a statute of limitations
between the saga of court battles and spoken word poems
between raising fist and picket signs and old hymns
the sounds of *semillas* given
their first drink of water in the earth

place this root on the tip of your palms
place this root on the tip of your tongue
place this root on the top of the next senate bill
place this root underneath your new house

SAND AND BONE DESERT SPARK

GABRIEL HARTLEY

Huesos arena spark
combine, conjunto
lost in the desert

burnt and callused feet
walking, hiding, running:

grain by grain the imprint
cry by cry the impact
trade agreement shipment of goods
more precious to the gods (capital)
than flesh (accident)

spark, phosphorescence, glimmer
what remains of lives given up
to the glow of memory—darkness

imprints in air and sand
their last breath
a suck of my own breathing
spin and dizzy the sand
sing and measure the sorrow

of a child at home now motherless
now fatherless
with only grain of bone of sand to testify
to the pull of love's immediacy
responsibility
and strength

blood and bone and sand
to the rhythm of riches and nations
spilled and spent

left to the spark of memory

JUAN MERCADO

RALPH HASKINS

An American,
born in a Texas town,
raised in a Mexican town,
both, mere feet apart,
separated by blood
and connected by blood.

Here the border blurs
beyond the river's banks
into an ethnic purgatory,
like a geography coloring book
the people crayoned
with their lives without staying
inside the lines.

With only Spanish
in his basket, he worked
the hot fields of Texas, picking
the grapefruits of his hard labor,

until the day the *migra* came.

Why should a man need
to prove his birth within
his country's citrus groves?
Amidst the ordered multitude
of trees that stood as witnesses
to an unjust incident
but remained silent for fear of being
ruled out of order by Sherriff Joe.

Juan was found
guilty until proven citizen,
declared "Undocumented Worker,"
illegal alien, thief
of another's employment,
and sentenced to exile,

this Juan Mercado,

this American.

Look at his brown skin! Listen
to his broken English!
He is just as American as Beck,
who recites his spotless CNN-glish
and whose document is
the whiteness of his skin.

KIM AYU (VENÍ PA'CA)

CLAUDIA D. HERNÁNDEZ

Mis entrañas se contraen

Es mi aliento que se escapa
Va en busca de mi gente

Oigo un eco que retumba
Voces dulces, lengua tierna:

Kim ayu — Vení pa'ca

Corre viento que me roza
Con olor a incienso

La marimba se oye lejos

Son los moros, han llegado
Con sus danzas de venados

Oigo un eco que retumba
Voces dulces, lengua tierna:

Kim ayu — Vení pa'ca

Los repiques de campanas en
Los templos siempre estallan

Ese acorde no se olvida

En mi piel cae la cera
Esta quema y hace llagas

Que me adiestran a apreciar
Una nueva existencia

Oigo un eco que retumba
Voces dulces, lengua tierna:

Kim ayu — Vení pa'ca

Mi alma ruge, ya no tiembla,
Ha encontrado al nuevo Edén.

WHERE WE BELONG

ANDREA HERNÁNDEZ HOLM

Arizona dirt, warm and thick
Place where I am rooted
Planted here because my *abuelos* had to choose
Which side of our mother's severed body
They would cling to.

They embraced Texas
Where the high desert didn't change
Just because there was a border
Where the river still carried their songs,
Where they could feel the heartbeat
Of the earth beneath them.

Until, tired of being
Mexicans Not Allowed
Mexicans Not Served
Mexicans Not Welcome
Mexicans Not Wanted
In stores, in schools, in lands
Where their bones and blood filled the earth,
Where they belonged,
They gathered up their sorrows and headed west.

Like *hormiguitas* pacing ancient paths,
Searching frantically for the scent of the familiar,
They found the long tunnel home here
In Arizona dirt, warm and thick.
And I'm not leaving now
Just because you want this land.

You say
Illegals Not Allowed
Illegals Not Served
Illegals Not Welcome
Illegals Not Wanted
And we hear the voices of long ago
Still shouting
Still trying to push us away.
But we are not leaving now
Just because you want this land.
We are already home.

IN RESPONSE TO THE MAN WHO ASKED, "WHY DO YOUR PEOPLE MARCH FOR EVERYTHING?"

ANDREA HERNÁNDEZ HOLM

We were marching long before
We even knew how to walk,
Before there was a notion of you or me —
Just a hope that there would be
One more generation of our people,
And another after that.

Our nanas marched us out of their wombs
To the rhythm of the drum
And we kept on marching, walking
Dancing, and singing
Until our praises were carried
In all directions
So that our ancestors would know we were here.

We march
Through sorrow and joy.
We march
When we are happy
And when we are angry.
We have marched from the belly of the earth
Through the deserts and mountains and rivers,
In the canyons and forests,
By the moonlight and the sunlight,
In the rain and the snow and the heat.

You can see the pattern of our journey
In the stars above.

We march until our voices are too weak
To sing us further.
We march until we are heavy with sweat.
We march to exhaustion.
We march until we bleed,
And still we march.

We make sense of the universe
When we march.
The pounding of our feet reverberates,
Returns to the life force
In all that surrounds us.

We do not march for ourselves.
We are only bodies of energy,
Our lives are but brief moments in time.
We march in the hope that there will be
One more generation of our people
And another after that.

ARIZONA GREEN (MANIFESTO #1070)

JUAN FELIPE HERRERA

For all those marching and writing against SB 1070 and for all those who
want to believe it
So it came to pass—

After the boycotts left the Arizona banks tortilla burnt and chipotle dry
After the boycotts shooed away the Republicans from the casinos and spas
After the boycotts jammed all the Holiday Inns the Westins and the rest
After the airports only served three-day old nachos
After the gun show tents frizzled into piñata bits
After all the lawns in Scottsdale rolled themselves up en route to Naco
After all the *turistas* popped a wheelie en route to Mesquite then El Paso
After all the jailbirds busted out singing *de colores de colores*
After all the city councils got bumped down by *los panaderos*
After all the mayors got spanked up by *las barrenderas*
After the last vigilante skipped out incognito as George López
After Governor Jan Brewer offered free workshops in *pendejismo*
After all the *bordo* walls and scanners and patrols shriveled and popped

Arizona went green
Arizona went green

Yes Arizona went absolutely green
Chile verde green
Celery and *lechuga* green
Jalapeño green serrano green
Broccoli green artichoke green green grape green
All those campesino greens all those greens
All those *folklórico* dress greens and *danzante penacho* bead greens

It was a kinda flowery Virgen de Guadalupe green
It was a kinda green you notice after an August monsoon storm green
It was a kinda green you notice after ICE agents zoom zoom out green
It was a kinda green you notice when you are runnin' illegal yes

You know the earth is with you
You know it because every day you touch it you speak to it
You say
with your cilantro-shaped voice You say
Eres todo lo que tengo

You are all I have
You say it because it takes a road ramblin' crossin' life to say it
You say it because it takes lost familia hands to touch it so you lift them
You join them with other hands even if they are miles away

That is when you dance
That is when you dance green in the green wind
That is when you dance green on the blown southern deserts of Arizona
Wild blades of green among the border dead
You rise again

Cilantronary:
• *los panaderos*, the bakers, givers of bread on your corner
• *las barrenderas*, the cleaning women, as in people's flags as in *banderas de la gente* green
• *pendejismo*, stupidity with a pen, a pen with Republican ink Inc.
• *bordo*, border as in the shape of an "¡Oh-rah-leh, chale!"
• *lechuga*, lettuce (ley-chew-gah, as in "let us," as in law, as in people's law)
• *campesino*, farmworker all amped up, *ampesino, ampesina, ampesin@* green
• *folklórico*, Chican@ Mexican regional dance group, feelin' good, a national green *zapateado* across community *centros* and schools and streets in Phoenix all the way to Tenochtitlán and beyond green
• *danzante penacho*, Aztec ceremonial dancer breastplate and a green pen, a feathery pen made of ceremonial stomps across the green *migrante* trails that erase all borders with green songs, green incense, and *puro corazón*.

A PRAYER TO SANTA CEBOLLA

MARI HERRERAS

Remember when your roots
tended our soil and your
tendrils caressed our hearts?

Santa Cebolla,
remember when we sat patiently,
waiting at the corner of your fields,
offering you our tears at harvest
pétalo a pétalo?

Today the soil has dried back into the caliche.
These tears are real as we sit together
and recall how we carried you with us
in hands
in baskets
through mountains, deserts, mesas
riverbanks, villages, cities

Pétalo a pétalo
we tell your stories to our children
of how you showed us true love,
protected us from sickness,
sent evil back to the fires

Pétalo a pétalo
now we pray to you
around kitchen tables where you sit
heaped on platters, a grilled offering
to remind us laughter and love are

reflected in each other's faces
despite how you left us behind to sing
our country, not our country
our history, not our history
our love, not our love

OUR CHILDREN ARE NOT ANCHORS

*"If we are going to have an effect on the anchor baby racket, we need
to target the mother. Call it sexist, but that's the way nature made it.
Men don't drop anchor babies, illegal alien mothers do."*
—Arizona State Senator Russell Pearce

SUSANA DE JESÚS HUERTA

Our children are not anchors
like those dropped in Atlantic waters to
unload African corpses en masse.

We don't just drop our babies
onto this land the way
bombs were dropped on
Hiroshima and
Nagasaki.

The way words and promises are dropped from treaties.

Our children do not drop like collapsed lungs
from smallpox in clean bodies under
wool blankets and thick air.

Our children are not the weights used
in that system of pulleys, noosed ropes over
oak and magnolia branches tied to
the gravity of brown and black bodies.

They do not fall hard like strong brown
soldiers on front lines holding
their breaths to be made
citizens while pledging patriotism and pride.

Our babies do not keep us
on these furrowed fields of crouching
backs under summer heat the way
threats to hire another force us to stay
even without running water, even without
a paycheck.

Our children are not anchors.

They do not fall.

They are already the root,
complex connections centuries old,
aflame with the power of history,
knowledge of collective pain and promise.

They become. They bloom. They unfurl like
lavender flowers and protest signs under desert
sun. Even as seedlings they grow beyond
the rubble of bones, poisonous policies
that sever family with barbwire borders.

Our children are the pulsating sky that sings
thunder and bleeds to break open and
burst forth like monarch clouds

returning home.

GRAVE SONG FOR IMMIGRANT SOLDIER*

José Gutiérrez, José Garibay, Diego Rincón, and Jesús Alberto Suárez were "green card soldiers" who died in Iraq and were given posthumous citizenship. Ezequiel Hernández was shot in the back while herding his family's goats near his home in Texas by Marines taking part in border maneuvers.

AURORA LEVINS MORALES

I am sitting right here in California this
occupied land ripped with borders,
borders running like red scars
under the city limits and county lines
stitched into our hearts with crimson threads
a thick embroidery of grief
welts of damage crisscrossing
the everyday landscape of ignorance.

The wealth of the world may enter
but its people may not.
Industrial-strength needles rise and fall
setting barbed wire stitches,
doing the meaty business of empire,
upon the hacked and reassembled body of the planet
drawing a bloody string through lives
that people living inside the gates
are instructed to forget

I am sitting here thinking Flor,
Germán, Lola, Manuel, Claudio,
Mercedita, Ricardo, Cristina, Ramón,
the stained gauze of foreignness
binding their fluid Caribe tongues.
I think how many Chinese women
were sent back yesterday morning
wrong papers start over
go back to sewing American flags
for six noodles a day
in mainland sweatshops
waiting for something new to happen.
I think Haitian bodies

---

*Note: This is an excerpt of a longer poem.

dark driftwood on Florida beaches.
I think how many miles
from San Miguel to Tombstone
if you go on foot.

They are playing taps
for José, Diego, Jesús Alberto, and José
sworn in with their mouths taped shut,
obscenely wrapped in the prize
they could only win by
going in front, falling first, dying fast.
They have been given their citizenship
in the cemetery of the star-spangled dead,
and their officers do not expect any trouble.
I tell them I cannot mourn you
in the small space they have set aside
in the margins of their blood road.
I must carry you with me.

I am thinking about Basra and the Alamo
about *Mayflowers* and leaky boats capsizing
downstream from Port-au-Prince, not pilgrims
about Arizona vigilantes with assault rifles
patrolling an invisible line at the edge of their fear
that runs right through our living rooms,
terrified that Michoacán will conquer Colorado
that bloodbath and bankruptcy will come home to roost
trying to hold their own history at bay with equipment.
I am trying to see the faces of the
ten thousand unnamed bodies
fallen into the gullies and canyons
of the crossing, the ones that are never found
and the two bodies a day they do find
strange fruit of the Mexican desert.

My great-grandmothers made lace,
twisting white cotton strands around pins
until the web could catch the sun, catch
a fall of jasmine down a wall,
delicate and tough, one thread bound into another,
spreading out across their beds and tables.
My great-grandmothers wound pain
around pins and fingers.

They made lace out of suffering
and I am unraveling bandages,
pulling weft from the fabric of lies.
I am trying to twist this savage thread
around the pins of what I know,
fastening this to that,
fraying the edges of nations
to make a blanket.

I am making a shroud for immigrant soldiers,
knotting and tying a thousand
journeys to locked gates,
going under and around,
doubling back, knowing that someone
traveled by night,
wore a disguise,
carried false papers,
swam the Ohio, the Mississippi, el Río Grande,
jumped a train,
crept through the sewers.
I am untwisting the sharp teeth of borders,
knitting rivers and veins in a fabric
as rough and fertile as earth,
the only cloth I can use
to bury you.

THE SAME THING

*"The trees on the mountain topple themselves
and the spring steals its own water."*
—Chuang 'zi

GENNY LIM

In comparing how prison camp workers
rubbed grains from ears of wheat stalks
and popped them in their mouths
it was every man for himself
recalls Er Tai Gao
who wore the dead man's coat
The young man had lied to his mother
that he was well, then died of starvation
wearing the blue coat she had made

In comparing our city's homeless
wearing rags that no one had made
and stuffing themselves with food scraps
rummaged from dumpsters and
the cold fire of whiskey
I wonder if captivity or freedom
amounts to the same thing?

Two deaths amount to one
When a mother awakens
in the dead of night
to discover the son she once nursed
has succumbed to the suckle of whiskey
Two deaths amount to one
when a mother awakens
in the chill of dawn to
discover her boy's letters from camp
have stopped for eternity

Two deaths amount to one
when the trees on the hillsides
can't lift the heavy rains that come
Two deaths amount to one
when the fish can't spawn upstream

because it's everyone for himself
and captivity and freedom
have become the same thing

THE REMEMBERED

GENNY LIM

We dream of the forgotten
When daylight breaks
we return to the shell of the living
We dream of the forgotten
whose yearnings spill into sunlight
We dream of the forgotten
whose faces are withered petals
whose names brush our lips
like blown candles
We dream of those we loved
of those we didn't, of those whom
we only knew in brief or in passing
through their footprints dogging our trail
through their songs trapped in our cells
through history's suffocating noose
through the jungle of paper bloodlines
to the altar of broken hearts

We dream of the forgotten because they
follow us through the skin of our memories
through the tracks of our journeys
through the unmarked graves of ancestors
through wars and exile
through births and deaths
through joy and sorrow
We dream of the forgotten because
they remember us
They inhabit us
They are us
They are the surf pounding rock
the battering sea shattered
into infinitesimal drops
Arching, wave after wave
against currents of migrating geese
We dream of the forgotten
as dispossessed lovers
who lived, who loved
like us

THE BORDER CROSSED US

MARK LIPMAN

I step onto land
where my ancestors
planted our family tree
over 1,000 years ago.

I have known no other sand
between my toes
under my feet
this is my only home.

One day though
a stranger arrived
sat down at our table
drank our wine
ate our bread
raped our women
burnt our village
then declared me illegal.

The color of my skin
the language on my tongue
the god that I chose to believe in
demonized in order to justify their cruelty.

The freedom that I enjoyed
my right to self-determination
gone, victim to yet another
military occupation.

My peace,
simply a broken olive branch
cut from the tree they tore down.

My home,
rubble beneath the tracks
of their bulldozers.

All I have ever had
all that I've ever known
all, taken from me.

My blood,
turned into their gold.

My heart,
broken from generations
of lies and betrayals.

If you cut me, do I not bleed?

Crushed, beneath the boot of technology
by persons with no soul or body to touch

with no heart to feel

eyes, blinded by hatred
ears, closed to any reason
mouths, shut out of fear

comfortably tucked away in their beds
while human beings die in the streets
under the batons and artillery shells
of a militarized police state.

Wrapping oneself in a flag
worse yet, a religion
while making excuses for genocide
sanctioning the murder of children.

News actors continue to blame the victims
force-feeding us lies, calling us terrorists
because we were born onto the land that they coveted.

Who is the real enemy,
the one who believes in something different than you,
or the one who uses what you believe in to change who you are?

There is no escaping the soul staring back in the mirror
regardless of the shifting lines on some map
human rights have no borders.

TRESPASSER SHOES

CÉSAR LOVE

Shoes perfect for the fastest dance
Shoes so cool
Even jaywalkers swoon.
Shoes that scale barbed wire
Two taps and you're invisible
To every cop and guard.
Shoes that violate the dress code
Shoes that never came in a box.
The shoes that skip over stairs
That short-circuit escalators
Three taps and you leap above
Foul lines, flag poles, border checkpoints.
Trespasser shoes
Polished with a darker shade of saint.
Hiding in your closet
Waiting to walk on water.

INSIST AND RESIST

MANUEL LOZANO

The old tradition knows the way,
its rebellious nature
will not lay down in the dust.
Se sacude las plumas
y levanta la cara
mientras estira sus alas
para volar.

Se rinde sólo al sueño
que comete el delito
of maintaining its pulse,
el de aquella infancia
en que toda inocencia
just refuses to tremble
before the ongoing nightmare.

This modern rendition
es la misma tormenta
Que estremeció la tierra
Hace más de quinientos
mechanized and updated.
Sus espinas de acero
culpables de tanto llanto.

I stand beside my carnalas.
I stand beside my carnales.
Beside all those soaring eagles
que son perseguid@s,
told it's their own fault
for being born in the shackles
of their beautiful brown skin.

Celebramos en canto.
Our song beats its drums
and shakes its serpentine rattles.
Insiste y resiste,
Y así aprendimos a sobrevivir.
Vamos y venimos,
El cielo y la tierra
nos lo ha permitido.

MY SWEET DREAM / MY LIVING NIGHTMARE: ADOBE WALLS

MANUEL LOZANO

What did I hear?
It is hard to describe,
The drums and the chanting
Of a beautiful tribe.
The flutes and the rattles,
Echoes and prayer—
The heartbeat of battles
Came out of nowhere.

I saw it all,
In one swooping brushstroke,
The vision was swirling
In the rising smoke.
The pendants were jaded,
Beaded and strung out,
We felt we made it
In the places we hung out.

The fragrance was rising
With a hint of delight,
And the moon in a crescent
Was hooked on the night.
I took in the perfume
As the starlight was gleaming,
And it was safe to assume
That the garden was dreaming.

The treble shook me,
And we rumbled through,
It felt like forever
Was looking like new—
Rugged and raw,
And we pounded along
With the clay and the straw
In the brick holding strong.

Oh, I could taste it,
The indigenous air,
With a hint of red earthenware clay,
And a magic so rare—
Now a living nightmare,
For the wild wind is blowing.

There was nobody there
When the rooster came crowing.

ON ISSUES OF ALIENS AND IMMIGRATION

DEVORAH MAJOR

1.
truth be told we are
all aliens now
traveling in outer space
on our rocky, blue sea planet

only a few of us stayed nestled
in the belly of our ancestors' birthing
on the lips our mother's womb

all of the rest of us have traveled
to here where our heads now sleep
to where our children grow and flourish
or wither and perish

but once we all were natives

long before the ones
whose names we have forgotten
began their trek

we all were natives

before the ones who stayed
stopped telling stories
of we who had left

eons ago we had no questions
about who was our kin

everyone was related

then we began to travel
turned each the other
into opposites
becoming and creating
aliens

2.
we traverse this planet
near the edge of our dark milky galaxy.
rotate steadily circling one sun
ghosted by one moon
in concert with no less than eight planets

we revolve with and without each other
some times meet meteors
who whistle through stardust
creating craters
sandstorms
lake beds
depositing minerals
and fossilized amoebas

and as we travel
comets sail by
their tails shimmering
hot smoky ice

and as we move past comets
moving past us
we see stars fall
from the sky and marvel
at being in the middle
of all these galactic wonders

thus we are traveling
with and as aliens
in outer space on this planet
where we live

and everywhere we stay
we are surrounded
by other voyagers
like and unlike us

i know
i've always been an outsider
amidst immigrants
beside aliens
next to strangers
just like you

THE LINE

JOHN MARTÍNEZ

Between two trees a line is drawn
But high in the sky
The diving birds
Witness their branches
Piercing clouds
To meet
And embrace

Soon their roots will tangle
Deep in the soil and fuse
So that eventually
Each tree has a bit
Of the other one's bark

The rain falls at an angle
The sun moves in precise time
Spreading rays on each tree

Between two trees a line is drawn
But this line is weak
Drawn with a pen
This line is temporary
As the wind
The rain
The scurrying leaves
The raising root
Will turn it back
Into the earth it was
And then
It will be gone

NUNCA, NUNCA, NUNCA

THE CORRIDO OF SOUTH PHOENIX

ANDREA GARCÍA MAUK

Nana sat by the window, rocked in her chair
Stared out at the street lined in orange blossoms
cada día, the same.
Recited her mantra, "*Nunca, nunca, nunca,*" and
Not one of us
Had any idea what she was trying to say.

First they took out her and Tata's house in Golden Gate
to make the airport stop busting its borders. To cut the tongues
from the novenas and Friday night sock hops at
Sacred Heart. To send the families fleeing
Their barrio, their birthplace, their history.

Then they silenced the Riverside, its shell still
Stands. If you press your ear to its walls, you
Might hear the music that was made, sense the
Rhythm in the feet of the people who danced there.
Feel it flow through you, a trace, a whisper, a hint.

Nana didn't stick around long enough to see
The day we returned to South Phoenix
And drove down Baseline Road to look
For the Japanese flower gardens that still
Smell so sweet in childhood memories made of
Blossoms, pink and yellow and lavender.

Miles of nothing where *tiendas* once stood.
They paved the dirt Euclid and erected lines of
two-story houses with pretty Spanish tiled roofs that
Obscured the views of the skyline, the mountains,
The past.

They tore down the borders they had put up around us
Back in the day when we were just kids.
They conquered their fears and traveled south
To stake the beauty of long forgotten outskirts

For their own.
But isn't that always how the story goes?

Nana sat by the window, rocked in her chair
Stared out at the street, lined in orange blossoms,
cada día, the same.
Recited her mantra, "*Nunca, nunca, nunca,*" and
Not one of us
Had any idea what she was trying to say. We
Thought she forgot, but now I wonder
If it was an inkling, a vision, the future she saw,
And bittersweet memory tearing her down.

ARIZONA GODDAM!

"Alabama's gotten me so upset
Tennessee made me lose my rest
and everybody knows about
Mississippi Goddam . . ."
—Nina Simone

JOSEPH MCNAIR

dos cabezas, yr steep mountain slopes and granite
outcroppings, yr vegetated canyon floors provoke
strong feelings of arousal, attraction, and yes,
even love by more than just the white-tailed and
mule deer or eagles, golden and bald, the ranging
mountain lion, the beautiful collared lizard and
the peregrine falcon. u, dos cabezas, are,
indeed, a love object for arizona natives
imprinted by the wilderness with its uncultivated
spaces, its searing heat with that eerie desert
dust on its winds, a narcotic that makes them
susceptible to quaint hallucinations (daylight
savings time is a bolshevik plot), conservative
and highly distrusting of government. (goddam!)
where lawmen under the influence of frontier
fancy could take a hapless but convenient
outlaw straight from the lyrics of their state
song, a befuddled recidivist burglar named
ernesto arturo miranda, compel from him a
rape, etc., confession, make him write it down
and sign papers with a printed certification that
he "voluntarily and of my own free will, with no
threats, coercion, or promises of immunity . . ." and
"full knowledge of . . . [his] . . . legal rights" made
that confession, but failed to inform him of
his right to have an attorney present and of his
right to remain silent. (goddam!)
where in a season that saw even ronald reagan
bow to the inevitable winds of change and sign
the king holiday into law, three house republican
arizonans, including an "unevolved" john mccain
and that doyen of true american conservatism,
senator barry goldwater, voted unequivocally no!

state lawmakers like sand lemmings followed suit.
babbitt, not sinclair lewis's vacuous protagonist,
but a governor doing the right thing, signed an
executive order declaring a paid king holiday.
but seven months and twenty-four days later, soon-to-be-
impeached evan mecham rescinded that order
in one of his first acts as governor! (goddam!)
rising from a searingly dry tropical air mass,
pulled northward by low-pressure cells moving
eastward across the two head's wilderness
echoing off the sulphur springs and the san simon
valleys came a venal and corruptible voice calling
out to arizonans with the arrogated authority of
i am that i am: "i guess king did a lot for the
colored people, but i don't think he deserves a
national holiday." but the rocks surely cried out
in protest and boycotts. all manner of stones,
pythagorean frozen music, released their song
with stevie wonder singing lead—happy birthday
to yuh—public enemy struck back, the nfl
relocated the super bowl and arizonans, kicking and
screaming, capitulated in '92. (goddam!)
where even the wind that competes at dusk
to be heard with the yips, barks, and howls of
coyotes in telltale yellow desert coats weeps and
wails in uncertain english even tho' placed for
a year in english immersion classes where
languages other than english were banned from
speech. brain-fried arizonans insist that the
speech of the alligator juniper, the bitter condalia
and crucifixion thorn, the catclaw, and even the skunk
bush had better be the same as that which arose in
england and southeastern scotland; that they
obsequiously subordinate their mother tongues,
their identity and culture, for to speak a language
other than english is nothing more than a social
defect. (goddam!)
behold arizonans, the behemoth that u have made,
rising out of the desert, so mean, and abrupt of
emotion—and so unlike that mighty torch-bearing
mother of exiles on a distant shore who verily
welcomed the poor and the homeless. this shire reeve
golem of single eye and foul disposition casts his

all-seeing searchlight glance to expose and extirpate
all illegals wherever they might be found, especially
in the ghostly golden gate barrio, in cuatro milpas,
or in any of the *barrios históricos* that housed the
brown laborers who built yr streets and towns, yr
canals, laid tracks for trolleys and trains that brought
in the droves of undocumented anglos who
overwhelmed the indigenous population! (goddam!)
what have u done, arizonans? the adam of yr labors
has run amok and points proudly back to the womb
from whence it came—that monster matrix of
racism, red-baiting, antigovernment sentiment, and
resentment of anything progressive, whose birth
juices reek of hatred and calumny—back to u and yr
guilt fear, yr paroxysmally parochial thinking. it has
engorged on a steady diet of rights violations, english-
only legislation, reasonable suspicion, and belief, and now
it stalks like a grotesquery seeking to devour the
interdisciplinary study of racialized peoples, latinos
and chicanos in particular. what makes u think, brain-
fried arizonans, that it won't turn on and devour u?

RIMAS CONTRA LAS CÁRCELES DE PAPELES

Para mis hermanitas(os) morenitas(os)

OCTAVIANO MERECIAS-CUEVAS

A ella le gusta surgir, sentir, decir, reír, escribir
Su día se describe entre surcos agrícolas de Oregón
Su historia es abnegada, ignorada por el blanco barrigón
sus sueños son ilegales en el mundo del anglosajón

No tiene papeles que puedan limpiar lágrimas de sus sueños
Sus amigas regresan del colegio el día de su cumpleaños
Y entre lunas sigue en el mismo campo esperando el día
Que la cobardía no triunfe sobre la misericordia.

Vive sin papeles entre ángeles, materiales de inglés
sueña que educando, escribiendo, leyendo se va doctorando
pero vuelve a la triste realidad de su identidad sin nacionalidad
otro día más como sombra en una tierra sin pluralidad.

Vuela, vuela palomita de papel, alas de miel,
Llévale al mandatario hojas arrancadas de su triste diario.
Que la sociedad vea las letras de su abecedario rutinario.
A diario, sus sueños son el motor de mi vecindario.
Este país solitario es beneficiario de su aporte comunitario.

THE GREAT WALL OF AMERICA

JAMES O. MICHAEL

We built a wall around this country . . .
a good five stories high.
If any hoser wants to climb it,
I'd like to see 'em try.

After we walled off Canada,
we built another wall down south,
from the California beaches
to the Rio Grandy's mouth.

All along our coastal shores,
we built enormous dikes,
anchored in the ocean floor
and topped with barbs and spikes.

We all gathered to admire our work.
The cash and effort that it took
to build this monstrous concrete wall
called for another look.

A little girl, aged five or six
asked with a puzzled grin,
"When you lock those people out,
don't you lock these people in?"

I must admit that girl was right.
I let out a mournful wail.
America's Great Wall had turned
our country into a jail.

THE DREAM THAT SLEEPS WITH POWER

A SONNET FOR THE DREAM ACT

"Soñar no cuesta."
—an old saying

EDITH MORRIS-VÁSQUEZ

I traveled the road of dreams and did not
know that it would come to an end but I
believed it would extend and always start
again and by its nature never die
or be detained. Dreams are not foreclosures,
bankruptcies, they're not bad deals behind doors
when economies decline, liberties abort,
and successes are judged by tallies of war.
How many of what origin are killed
in a day, how proud and patriotic
is death's banner? Dark, dry, and deserted
the dead end of dreams sad and symbolic.
It's not just the dollar that's lost its hour
now dreams are only for those in power.

ANCIANOS

YASMEEN NAJMI

I ask the ancestors to help me
be the smoke from incense
that burns in their name
the silver-streaked braids
of our Mother Blue River
sliding through brown fingers
the rustling of cottonwoods
bloodletting the sun
as it fires volcanoes
we are these streams
traceable and fed
carving, carrying your landscapes
you sent Blue Heron
to show me how to be
water and wind
a stormy spot that appeared
a piece of waning sky
or the Sandias fallen
like you, who always caught us as we fell
and raised us to the sky.

HAIKU POEMS FOR SOCIAL JUSTICE

JOE NAVARRO

social justice wept
with sorrow song *lágrimas*
in Arizona

winds of social change
swept over Arizona
shedding some light

leftover garbage
from annexation era
filled Arizona

darkness fell upon
backs of hardworking people
crushing their spirits

even cops said no
when they heard the news about
stopping Mexicans

hope is tomorrow
when yesterday has been lost
a fresh start coming

oppression dies when
people cry with tears of hope
for social justice

Arizona
is not Jan Brewer, of course
which leaves room for hope

Arizona is
America, don't you see?
we've got work to do

travel and work laws.
unfair immigration laws.
open borders now!

GHOST TOWN

24 HOURS B4 ARIZONA'S SB 1070

GERARDO PACHECO MATUS

Doña Rosa left early this morning.
She loaded everything she owned in her car
and said good-bye to us. She went to Utah.

The little girls from the house next door
don't cry anymore. Yesterday, their mothers
took them away. They're heading to Chicago.

The school, up the hill, is empty.
The few children who stayed today
are not coming back tomorrow.
They'll leave with their parents tonight.

Mr. and Mrs. Ramírez left last night.
They planned to drive all night until
they reach San Francisco. I believe
their children live up there in La Mission.

Don Goyo sold all of his farming tools
and bought a one-way ticket to New Mexico.
He has a son over there. He'll be okay.

Los Pachecos told me they'll leave
as soon as they fix their old Beetle,
and if they can't fix such an old thing,
they'll hit the road anyways . . .

Chucho, *el carnicero*, didn't open
his *carnicería* today. I couldn't buy *carne
de puerco*. I waited for him this morning,
but I think he's gone too.

Rosita, *la tamalera*, is gone. She used
to stand on the corner selling her tamales
dulces, but I'm afraid she left too.

The church bells didn't toll this morning.
I think El Padrecito left early too. He must
have gone to his small village in México.

Everybody from La Bendición de Dios has left.
They all told me they'll come back soon,
but *la pinche* SB 1070 *está cabrona*.

La pinche SB 1070 is only hours away.
Man, I've to get out of here.
I need to hit the road too, or else
hasta México puedo ir a dar.

OUTLAW ZONE

MELINDA PALACIO

Arizona
lull me back
to sun rays on mountains,
full moon hikes and coyote cries,
heat from windless days, where
people dared build
cities in a desert.

Don't piss me off, Arizona,
Don't go back to those ugly years
of no Dr. King days with your
sweeps and roundups,
sounds like a rodeo, *¿qué no?*
Don't prey on your people, gente
browner than an Arizona sunset.

Shoes, you say.
You can tell by their shoes.
Shoes say it all:
inmigrante, illegal.

Don't tell me where you came from
or how the West was won
or why you think Arizona,
land of little water, chollas,
bottlebrush sage, ocotillos, saguaros
is only for those whose skin burns pink.

Arizona,
Add air to your name,
Air-uh-zone-uh. Air-a-
zone for legals,
ahh-ry-zo-naaa.

Arizona,
Don't forget which country you come from.

FADING MEMORIES

CARLOS PARADA AYALA

I want to sing of mangoes dangling in bunches,
ripening in branches of massive trees,
swaying in the orchards like sweet grandmothers in a dream.

I want to sing of cashew fruit sparkling red and yellow
shortly before noon under the nurturing sun of the equator.

I want to sing of bands of parrots dashing the sky
with brightly colored feathers against a canvas of puffy white clouds.

I want to sing of spider monkeys frolicking among the guavas,
startled by the sudden presence of a curious boy.

I want to sing of bougainvillea and croton bushes
decorating my field of vision as I walked in awe on my way to school.

Instead I sing of soldiers fighting in unwanted battles
among crying children and fearful mothers.

I sing of mental patients begging for mercy
in the streets of wealthy cities.

I sing of workers crossing borders,
braving foul rivers and border patrols
for a better life just beyond the horizon.

I sing of young men, lost in time,
while making time in federal prisons.

Yes, I want to sing, I want to rejoice,
but instead I cry out and protest
while the echoes of guavas and spider monkeys
fade in my memory like nostalgic creatures starving for attention.

I AM AMERICA

RAMÓN PIÑERO

I am America
from the
tundra to
Patagonia

from the
wheat fields
in Kansas
to the orange
groves in
Florida

I am America
from
New York
to Cuzco
from
Buenos Aires
to
Eagle Pass

I am America
my sweat
built the
railroads
I left
my blood
in Panama
in a canal

I am America
from Machu Picchu
to Tenochtitlán
from Quintana Roo
to Appalachia

I am America
I left
my body
on the Trail of
Tears

I am America
I died on the
Bataan Death March
and in the mountains of
Argentina

An Aztec
took my
still beating
heart and raised
it to the
heavens

I am America
I sleep in
a dead-end
alley
covered by
cardboard

I am America
I watched the
fires in Detroit
and in the
Bronx
I died at
Wounded Knee
I spent my
early youth
in Manzanar

I am America
I conked
my hair
in the fifties
and wore
dashikis and
a 'fro
in the
sixties

I was
one of the first
to die
in Vietnam

I am America
I am that
hillbilly
who
sees
that the
boot
on my
neck
is the
same as
the boot
on yours

I am America
I rode
with
Geronimo
Bolívar
and
Louverture

I died
in the
Ponce massacre

I am America
I followed
the fruit
and the
vegetables

La caña
in
Belle Glade
El tomate
in Ruskin
la lechuga

in *el Valle*
y la uva
también

I am America
United Fruit
and Dole
know
me by name

I am America
I sat with
Malcolm
and Martin
I drank
coffee
with Martí
and Don Pedro

I am America
from the
Aleuts
to
Tierra del Fuego
from the Andes
to the
Florida swamps

I am America
I made
Columbus
famous
for all
the wrong
reasons

I am
that baby
in a dumpster
that junkie
on the
streets
you walk

by me
and
cannot
see me

You call
me many
different
names

spic
injun
redneck
nigger
greaser

I am
not
hyphenated

I am America!

REASONABLE SUSPICION

MANUEL RAMOS

The people defined
by reasonable suspicion
are everywhere
without
being anywhere

and that's suspicious

Viejita hunched
over loads of
dirty hotel laundry
stands as short
as my impossibly short
grandmother

Young roofer
with insolent walk
wears my father's nose
as though they were brothers
from the same regal line
of kings and warriors

so suspicious

Joke-telling scrubber
of the Pollo Rico grill
could be my cousin
if my cousin
had lived
through 'Nam

Laughing girl
cleaning toilets
spooks me
with eyes
that must have been
stolen from my mother

very suspicious

Daily encounters
with familiar strangers
do not subdue the hate
or calm the hard wind
and we are, again,
the usual suspects

Arizona drowns
in sands of suspicion
as it denies
reflections
of my family
as saviors

WHO CARES?

MARITZA RIVERA

Family secrets:
who is legal, who is not.
We're all related.

HERE TO STAY

MARITZA RIVERA

I am the brown face
of immigration reform
that is here to stay.

SIN FRONTERAS

MARITZA RIVERA

¿Qué hay que hacer hoy
para crear la paz en nuestro mundo?
Vivir sin fronteras.

BEYOND BORDERS

MARITZA RIVERA

What must we do now
to create peace in our world?
Live beyond borders.

DILUYAMOS LAS FRONTERAS

MARGARITA ROBLEDA

No vine nomás hasta aquí
pa' hacerte la guerra,
ni pa' robar tu ganado,
ni pa' volarte la novia,
ni pa' colarme en la noche,
como un ladrón cualquiera.

Vine a darte mi mano,
pa' que juntos
construyamos la casa,
y que unidos,
inmigrantes casi todos,
junto con los herederos,
inventemos a esta gran nación.

No me pidas que me hinque
ni que agache la cabeza,
no esperes que te suplique,
ni que humille a mi descendencia;
que pa' eso tengo bien presente
quienes fueron mis abuelos:
talentosos arquitectos,
matemáticos brillantes,
que hasta inventaron el cero.
Artistas, artesanos,
hombres y mujeres de bien;
alegres, trabajadores y cariñosos;
astrónomos y sacerdotes.
También, pa' que negarlo,
hombres águilas,
caballeros tigres:
feroces guerreros.

Sí, las fronteras
las inventaron los hombres,
que los hombres las derriben;
que una sola es la casa,
una sola es el alma.
Y si una sola es la tierra,

una sola, también,
es la herida.
Que seres humanos somos todos
sin importar el color.
Y si una es la sangre . . .
¿Por qué no podemos pedir
que sea uno solo el corazón?
¿Que nos llamemos hermanos,
hermanas,
que compartamos el pan,
la alegría y el dolor?
Yo quiero darte mi canto,
mi risa y mi cultura de más de 5,000 años;
quiero aprender de ti
constancia, tenacidad,
tu capacidad de prever el futuro;
quizás,
hasta un poquito,
un cachito tan sólo . . .
de tu cordura.

Noche y día,
día y noche,
que dancen las estrellas,
que suenen los cascabeles,
que hoy estamos de fiesta;
que la tierra es de todos.
¡Viva la independencia!
Sin importar las lenguas;
que el respeto
sea el salvoconducto
que diluya las fronteras.

Sabemos que el que se cierra, pierde;
que la conciencia de ello
nos permita reencontrarnos
y derribe nuestras barreras:
las tuyas, las mías,
las de los mercaderes,
las del egoísmo,
las del miedo,
las de los gobernantes,
las del hambre.

No vine nomás hasta aquí
pa' robarles nada . . .
Vine a compartirles la vida:
el sudor, la sangre,
el cariño,
la alegría,
los sueños
y la esperanza.

THAT INDIAN MAN YOU SEE ON THE HOSPITAL BED

ROBERTO CINTLI RODRÍGUEZ

That Indian man you see on the hospital bed
he is eighty-seven years old.
He affectionately is known as Miracle Man.
That Indian man
on the hospital bed
has lived twenty-five years beyond the time
he was administered his last rites.
That brown man
has but a third grade education.
I have a PhD
yet he knows much more than me . . .
And all that I know,
he taught me.
That man is my father.
Some say he rambles on incoherently
but they seem not to know his memories.
He speaks of migrations
ancient migrations
from north to south.
"From somewhere here from
the United States."
And ones to El Norte,
from south to north.
He speaks of his own migrations
from Tenochtitlán
from Mexico City
to Aguascalientes to Chicago
to Los Angeles, California.
And our migrations
from Aguascalientes to Tijuana
to Los Angeles.

Chicago is where he would have settled,
where we would have been raised,
if not for his compadre
who took a train to Los Angeles.
In his mind, he goes back to the days

before his migrations
when he worked at the railroad,
with his brother
in Aguascalientes
whose elders told him that when
he decided to move to El Norte,
to show them that
"Mexicans know how to work."
He goes further back,
revealing the source of his learning
from his father
who taught him
the way he taught me.
That man on the hospital bed
is a carpenter,
a master carpenter.
He is a worker,
worked all his life.
Never less than two jobs
at a time,
often three.

Worked all his life with his hands
and his keen mathematical mind.
See that man on the hospital bed?
He also was a dancer . . .
"Floors cleared when he danced,"
my mom always said.
And true enough . . .
even on their sixtieth anniversary,
the floor cleared when he danced,
when they danced
as if it were the '40s.
That man on the hospital bed,
he can barely move now,
he can barely breathe.
Yet I can still see him dance.
My mind drifts to a time before my time.
I can see him in his *tacuche*,
in his zoot suit, along with his brother.
And I can see the floors clear as he danced
boogie-woogie and swing.
This from a photo in his sister's house

in Aguascalientes
never seen in Los Angeles.
That man in the hospital bed,
he still recognizes me.
He looks dazed,
but he still recognizes those he has known all his life.
When I look at him
it's as if I'm looking at a mirror
but a mirror, not of reality,
but of time.
When I see my own reflection in windows
I see that Indian man
the same one on that hospital bed.

He is me
or I am he
the same DNA.
When I sit next to him
I hold his hand
I reassure him that I love him
that we all love him.
He understands me,
he is conscious.
He looks at me.
His eyes tell me
he comprehends
the significance of this moment.
This has never happened before
in my fifty-six years.
I tell him that we all owe him,
that we all owe everything to him,
to him and my mother,
who both raised us, first in Aguascalientes,
then in Tijuana,
where I still remember his visits from Los Angeles,
then East LA, then later Whittier, California,
where he finally bought a three-bedroom home
with avocados,
this after thirteen years of eight of us,
then nine of us
living in a two-room shack
in an alley in East LA.
That man on the hospital bed

is having trouble breathing,
having trouble swallowing his food.
He chokes,
can barely breathe.
But he lives,
he survives.
His will to live is unfathomable.
It is deep and profound.
He fights like he has fought his whole life.
He has instructed us not to pull the plug,
he wants to be resuscitated.
At night, he sleeps.
He slips in and out of consciousness.
His body twitches.
He looks at me.
I hold his hand.
"I love you,"
I tell *mi papá*.
I can say this now.
Could not say this twenty-five years ago.
I could never say this before,
ever.

Two days ago
he was once again administered his last rites.
Drove all night to see him once again.
Drove all night
from Tucson to Brownfield, Texas,
where the letters *KKK*
are chiseled into the building
next to City Hall.
Drove all night to see him once again,
slept on the side of the road
three times,
pitch black sky.
Had to get there safely.
Should be driving to LA,
to Whittier,
but they're no longer there.
Drove all night in the opposite direction.
Had to face my mortality.
Was I driving to see him
or to see myself?

To face myself?
For him
or for myself?
To show him my love,
my appreciation,
or to clear my conscience?
Things cannot be undone.
I still have memories of a brutal childhood.
Yet now,
my memories of a guiding father,
of a storytelling father,
are stronger,
are more important.
That Indian on the hospital bed
transmitted knowledge and
passed on to me his memories.

Long ago
and minutes ago.
Passed on the stories of those ancient migrations
when I was a child
and when I was doing my PhD.
I created a diploma
for my father and for my mother
and for all the elders who contributed
their knowledge for my PhD.
He passed on to me his memories
the memories that go back
thousands of years.
It is what I came to call
"Ceremonial Discourse."
From parent to child.
He learned from his father
(José)
as he learned from his.
He taught me.
He passed down his memories
his knowledge
from father to son,
ancestral knowledge,
and reminded me that I did not grow up
knowing the *maíz* or the *frijol* . . .
the precise topic of my dissertation.

That was part of the story of the migrations
so that we not know the backbreaking work
of the campo,
of the fields,
the backbreaking work in our memory.
And yet, it is he who relayed the stories
relayed the memories,
of being of this land.
Not from across the oceans.
"We didn't swim across the ocean to get to El Norte,"
he instructed me as a child.
He also taught me,
instructed me never to stop eating chile,
lest I lose my tongue.
There's something about the chile.
Maíz without the chile is like . . .
Life is unimaginable without it.
That man on the hospitable bed,
he has lived with Alzheimer's and dementia
for twenty-five years.
More severe, the past several years.
But he is not incoherent.
More than ever,
he makes total sense.
More than ever, he is completely coherent.
His life has meaning.
It's all around him
his children
those close to him
his grandchildren and great-grandchildren.
He is not alone
nor abandoned.
His life has meaning.
It is said he was an orphan
but how could that be so
if his life has meaning?
That Indian man
who taught me to defend myself (my culture)
who taught me who I am
will live forever.

I drove all night
so I could tell him once again

to tell him
to hold his hand for the first time
to tell him, and let him know that I love him
that I follow his footsteps
that I continue the migrations
that I honor
that I carry within me
his memories
his father's memories
the ancient memories
my memories
his spirit
my spirit
Somos Uno
San Ce Tojuan
We are One
In Lak'ech
Tú eres mi otro yo
Papá,
soy tú

LO PROHIBIDO

ICE states its mission: to protect national security, enforce immigration laws, fight crimes and terrorist activity.

RENATO ROSALDO

In Manhattan, the phone woke me.
My daughter, Olivia, called from Oakland,
told me what José, her fourth-grade student,
told her that morning. Face flushed, eyes wide,
he spoke only Spanish, *el idioma*
en que pudo decir lo prohibido.
On his way home from César Chávez Elementary School
in Richmond, the *migra* called ICE, asked,
Who in your house has no papers?
I'm a citizen, born here, the boy said.
As José arrived home,
the *migra* burst in,
dogs straining on leashes.
The boy's eyes fixed
on jaws, snarls, white teeth.
His family has papers,
but in five days, José will be sent
back to Mexico, where he's never been,
the walk home from school without dogs.

BRATACHA BÁNA

GABRIEL ROSENSTOCK

Tá bratach Mheiriceá
ar an ngealach
iompaithe bán,
tuartha ag an ngrian.
Ní faic anois iad
na réaltaí, na stríoca,
brionglóid.

Lá breá gréine
is beidh gach brat tréigthe

WHITE FLAGS*

GABRIEL ROSENSTOCK

The American flag
on the moon
has turned white,
bleached by the sun.
The stars and stripes
are nothing now,
a dream.

Some sunny day
all flags will be that way.

---

*Note: Translated from the Irish by the poet.

BANDERAS BLANCAS*

GABRIEL ROSENSTOCK

La bandera americana
en la luna
se ha vuelto blanca,
desteñida por el sol.
Las estrellas y barras
son nada ahora,
un sueño.

Un día asoleado
todas las banderas se harán así.

---

*Note: Spanish translation by Francisco X. Alarcón.

IF YOU LEAVE YOUR SHOES

JOSEPH ROSS

If you leave your shoes
on the front porch
when you run

to the city pool
for swimming lessons,
you might end up

walking across the sand
of the desert in
scorched feet,

bare, like the prophets,
who knew what it was
to burn.

If you leave your lover
to run to the market
for bread and pears

you might return
to find your lover
gone and the bed

covered with knives,
hot and gleaming from
a morning in the sun.

If you leave your country
in the wrong hands,
you might return to

see it swimming in blood,
able to spit
but not to speak.

CHOOK SON, ARIZONA

Mitakuye Oyasin

ABEL SALAS

Palabra de mis primos Pimas
'cuz ya know Cuahuiltecas
y Mexicas came for trade
and water from the black
creek like a diamond snake
símbolo de parientes y
descendientes de Quetzalcoatl
so what if your paranoid
rancheros who fled San Joaquín
and a storm-trooper rabid
dog sheriff akin to Himmler
whose name is on a page
next to the governor who
signs the legislation that
labels you all forever as
paranoid Neanderthals
will soon be unable even to
communicate with your
own grandchildren for
fear of a bilingual nation
brown and proud, a nation
that honors the Apache
warriors who fought hard
and fast for a desert
homeland security you
could not nor would not
fathom because the rocks
and the mesquite did not
welcome you with love.
Inside your own hearts you
know the brutality which
you feel you must inflict on us
to protect a way of life
that is a vapor slowly fading.
Óyeme bien, Arizona, más que
tu mitad es mi brazo y mi
herencia. My family has

harvested cotton in Casa
Grande for as long as I
can remember. And my
father's nephews have
made camp and compromise
with your redneck yahoo
truck stop regulars for near
half a century. That steel
sprung Mixteca standing
alongside a Zapoteca and
a Maya who are willing to
work from sun up to sun fall
are the clave to your only future
but you have become so
dim-witted and angry you can only
answer with violence and
reprimand, take away the
books and the plática that
will make your young ones
free and full. We do not seek
an overthrow or a coup, 'cuz
we know how to share. We've
been doing it for 15,000 years
in Tucson and across the two
continents you invaded with
bloodshed and greed from
across an ocean like pillagers
in your storied Viking plunder
pride legends, the same ego
that made some among you
imagine a master race and
liquidate artists, truth tellers,
singers, and sacerdotes who
were not like you. Be assured,
Arizona es nuestro, and your helpless
hold on a reality that evaporates
more each day is the epitome
of lo precario. I wish I could feel
more sympathy and empathy
but I'm too busy learning and
teaching ethnic studies by virtue
of my simple existence. Nuestras
voces se unen y no nos puedes

callar aunque te parezca una
pesadilla de las peores.
Welcome to 2012, where we
will wait with a warm cup of
xocolatl just for you in the
name of peace and harmony.

PRAISE TO ALL THE POETS RESPONDING TO SB 1070

RAÚL SÁNCHEZ

Behind the great wooden gate
screeching past the threshold
our memories blossom into the open air
under the blue star-spangled sky
our cultures united
tapestry of colors, accents
flavors, *café con leche*
black and white
Cuba, Mexico, Venezuela, Colombia
Borinquen bella, escuchen mi llanto
la patria aquella que se ve de lejos
y se siente cerca
Argentina, Chile, Paraguay
far away yet near
our thoughts *y pensamientos* connect
the place of being with the state of mind
our cultures bring together
family lasting friendships
our cultural bond strengthened
our voices connected
with dignity and respect
aligned in culture and pride
poets, writers, artists
love for *la Raza*
united in this land
to the north
we are all Americans
we are just another shade of brown
living *en El Norte,* north of Aztlán.

DENIAL

MATT SEDILLO

Prodigal sons often return
To feasts and celebrations
While prodigal grandchildren
Far too often arrive
Mid–funeral procession . . .

Like most things in my life
I arrived to my
Grandfather's final days
In denial
Last we spoke
He lay gasping for air
Forgetting his English
Me regretting the years
Of distance that
Had broken my Spanish
Trying to remind him
Of a little house in
The backyard he
Had built for his grandchildren
Recuerde
Viejo
La casita
Para los niños
Que . . .
Con tus manos
I couldn't find the words
As his eyes would soon close
His lungs soon too choke
I wanted to close in
Close the distance
I wanted to change the past
These past few months
I wanted to have been there
To be here but then
I wanted him to understand
I wanted to be understood
But I couldn't find the words
As he lay there just beyond

My grasp
So I could see
Shortest distances
Are the cruelest
And when he passed
I couldn't help but feel
Cornered trapped by people
Who shared their feelings freely
Who wanted to cry with me
But I wanted to be gone
Away from mothers
Uncles, aunts, cousins, family
I wanted miles of distance
From anyone who knew this man
Because I live in denial
And I wanted that back

As she lost her father
I couldn't look into
The eyes of my mother
The woman who had
Given me life
Mourning the death
Of her last surviving parent
Of her last living lineage
Of what came before her
I could not look into the eyes
Of my mother
But I had to and I have to
Because she is my mother
And he was my grandfather
And this is my family
And I cannot deny that
And I cannot be distant

Live
Like a loving thing
Love
Like a living thing
Let your love ripen
Like a grape on vine
And cherish
The ones you love

Every day
In the same way
As you would
As they lay dying

BE FEARLESS: CHOOSE LOVE

To Jessica Xiomar García and Camilo Landau

NINA SERRANO

Afraid of computer viruses
Afraid of terrorists
Afraid of the planetary extinction
of our current paths
of spreading diseases
of urban crime rates
drug lords owning governments
torture as a commonplace weapon
and humanless drones
with only a button to press
to explode life to smatters and splinters
only a law to pass to steal it all

Fearless love is the only defense
to face the morning light
Greedy power in my face like in yours
wants to make us forget
But we cannot forget this nagging feeling hardwired in the bones
wanting to belong snugly
in the nest of our planet
be accepted fully because we exist
and not for our documents, licenses, and wealth
From that innate primordial desire comes our fearless love
peeking around the polluted rubble of destruction
the abandoned gas stations the poisoned waterways
We look beyond and see other heads bobbing up
and down
beaming the signal
calling to us to show our fearless love
in the face of everything
Fearless love the daily challenge
Ready or not
it is here

DESAPARECIDOS

TOM SHELDON

Your changes have been saved.
The ghosts of immigrants prowl the hills.
They are not wholly forgotten,
they do not die but remain
within the soft folds of the earth,
amidst the ash of twilight fires
separation and longing.
Unsure of the way home,
whispering down dusty alleys
wind blowing trash in the dawn
a voice sounds from the desert
a soulful reminder of how alone they are,
cradled in the safety of death.

THE SACRED STONE

HEDY GARCÍA TREVIÑO

I went tonight in search
of sacred space.

I placed the final stone
beneath the moon
of falling leaves.

I heard the cry of our people
in the distance
I saw the cloud storm
gather near
I see the smoke rising.

But the river song
calmed my heart.

The sunset star
called forward the moon
and lit the pathway
to rainbow mountain
where the blanket of life
will embrace us.
And gather us from the storm.

Our journey will not end like
feathers in the wind
or like songs of sorrow.

The ancient ones will
guide us though the fire.

When morning dawns
the sun
will call our name
and the hills will sing in celebration.

The sacred circle
will bring us home again
like sacred herbs in bloom.

We will arrive in Springtime once again
disguised as hummingbirds and butterflies.

The ancient routes are imprinted like stardust
in our dreams.

In full flight we will celebrate the light
and feast upon the blossoms of our labor.

SEVEN EARS OF MAIZE I DO BRING

HEDY GARCÍA TREVIÑO

There between the sounds of sorrow
on red hilltops far from the sea

Bring forth the bells and the rattles
evoke the rain from the clouds

Harvest the songs of Chicomecoatl
walk in the river of time

Seven ears of maize
I do bring

Harvesting memories
whispering melodies

There between the rows of maize
I hear the song of the Corn Goddess

Seven ears of maize I do bring

There with bare feet planted
in soft warm earth

There in *la milpa* with arms stretched toward the sun
under ocher clouds

Seven ears of maize I do bring

Adorned in your glory Chicomecoatl
Sustain me oh Corn Goddess

I am maize
I am the dew on a cool morning

Growing roots
and waiting for the harvest

Seven ears of maize I do bring

BORDERS

TARA EVONNE TRUDELL

borders
everywhere
lines drawn
telling us
where to stand
to serve
to exist
to call ourselves
to die
borders
with guards
trigger-happy
shoot to kill
don't cross back
to the motherland
don't know your roots
confused by the terms
building borders in your mind
it's not Hispanic
it's not Spanish
it's not Latino
it's the Mexican blood
the Indian blood
that has been drained
into the land
the home
of my heart
my ancestors
my roots
my soul that knows
no borders

ARIZONA LAMENTATION

LUIS ALBERTO URREA

We were happy here before they came.

This was always Odin's garden,
a pure white place.
Cradle of Saxons,
birthplace of Norsemen.

No Mexican was ever born here
until their racial hatred and envy
forced us to build a border fence.
But they kept coming.

There were never Apache villages here —
we never saw these Navajos, Papagos,
Yaquis. It's a lie. Until their wagons
kept coming and coming. And their soldiers.

We worshipped at the great god's tree.
We had something good here.
We had family values and clean sidewalks.
Until those savages kept coming, took our dream

and colored it.

AZ SB 1070

STALKING THE DIVINE UNDER A DESERT FULL MOON

PAM USCHUK

1.
Bleached as the bones of migratory birds, broken
stones powder the foothills above Phoenix's million lights.
What shadows mark the true currency
of freedom's long journey into the divine?

The arms of saguaros rise like so many immigrants
pinned to the night sky, twisted and begging
stars from the deaf hands of gods
whose language of NO clicks like bullets shoved
into the asphyxiated chambers of ignorance and disdain.

2.
We are not afraid of rattlers,
refugees whisper to crushed granite
that doesn't believe them,
not afraid of the sidelong skitter
of the fanged tarantula looking for a mate
or the gila monster, its hide beaded
as a bag slung over the bare shoulder of a night queen.

We are not afraid of javelinas who materialize
to stampede, clattering through creosote bushes
on either side of our legs, they say,
knowing their skin is vulnerable
as tears smearing *la migra*'s indifferent fists.

3.
How did they finally arrive in this place
from the slums of Nogales,
the empty stomach of Guerrero
or busted maize farm in Chiapas?
Stars shatter like the headlights of Border Patrol trucks
on impact with their starving shoulders
at the edge of infrared sights.

Desert wind scours this emptiness,
a lockjawed wind disguised as law
emptying hatred like molten tar
into calluses pocking poor hands
offered to this country's needs.

4.
We do not fear the owl, heavy horned
and menacing a mesquite, owl landing
like a small boulder thrown into lacy limbs, owl
whose eyes are chiseled from yellow ice,
asking who,
who, who is next?

5.
Blue dwarfs spin near Scorpio poised
to sting the southern horizon
where moon lifts her saffron robes
into acetylene white, blind
as the scald of searchlights on a child's terrified face,
blind as the metal bite of handcuffs
on a father's wrists, blind as
a mother's belief in a better life for her kids.

6.
Walking the desert, we learn
our places, learn the strict edicts
of talons and venom, of wild pigs
who materialize to surround us, popping
scimitar teeth, slitting thighs
and torsos to bare ribs, learn
finally that borders
are merciless as the promise of safe haven
and the avenging angels of governors
that snuff out the small songs of our lives.

We do not fear any of them.
Moon, oh moon, we do not shrink
from your luminous heart
transforming desert dust to silver.

As you ascend the nexus of dark, teach us
to flex our new wings
which can never be legislated
even when our tongues offend commands
that would extinguish our common human blood.

NO CONSOLATION FOR LIDIA

NORMA LILIANA VALDEZ

above and below
late summer

insatiable thirst
for rivers grand

rattling of
desert canyons

empty bottle
found in sagebrush

coyotes howl
amid scrublands

mother abandoned
to triple digit temperatures

only her hand recognizable
in the blaring

silence of ruptured hearts

FOR A FRIEND WHO OBJECTS TO COMPARING THE EVENTS LEADING UP TO THE HOLOCAUST WITH WHAT IS HAPPENING TODAY IN ARIZONA

"I'm marked by the color of my skin. / The bullets are discrete and designed to kill slowly. / They are aiming at my children. / These are the facts."
—*from "Poem for the Young White Man Who Asked Me How I, an Intelligent, Well-Read Person, Could Believe in the War Between Races," by Lorna Dee Cervantes*

RICHARD VARGAS

for you "never again"
is personal and sacred
never again to being reduced
to less than human
never again to madmen
who spit their words
at you like careless
but calculated grenades
never again to being
scapegoat while a
government dulls
the minds and hearts
of its citizens to accept
the atrocities it will do
in their names

but even as i read this
we both know
it is
happening again
all over the world
and now
within our own borders
the tribes are different
yet they are the same
the raging wall of flame
that almost consumed
your people still burns
aided by strong winds

flapping the flags of old
and new hatreds

it's a modern-day
pogrom in the making
fingers pointing at "illegal
aliens" and "anchor babies"
words devised to strip
away humanity from
the powerless

but you and i know
what's really going on
the names of brown people
are being redacted
from our children's
history books
right now

we both know this beginning
this beginning with an end
no one wants to think about
but dwells deep inside our
fear gnawing nonstop like
a shiny slick maggot

so let us use your words
your gift to the world
language to name
the unspeakable
the unimaginable
the horrible

we will stand together
shout them out with
your same passion
and defiance in the
face of this heartless
beast

never again
never again
nunca más

EMIGRO

CARLOS VÁZQUEZ SEGURA

Emigro de aquí
de mí, del hijo que soy
y de los que tengo.

Emigro
cual ave hambrienta
del hielo intestinal
del invierno perenne
que me atrofia
el miedo.

Emigro al vacío;
al buitre
del moribundo;
al oso del salmón
para desovar la culpa
en la que he nadado
toda posible miseria.

Emigro
a donde nadie verá
en mis ojos
arena del recinto
que derrumbo al irme.

Emigro
a diluir mi nombre
en la masa ilegal
inmune al ojo
de miope derecho.

Me voy de mí, de aquí
al patio del infierno
que ya me apunta
detrás del río.

LOS DESAPARECIDOS

EDWARD A. VIDAURRE

Everyone has the gift of invisibility,
even the border wall goes unnoticed in June after a
month that drains us of life. The scent of knives
on a hot summer day is the only constant
amongst the news of *frontera* tragedies and a poetry
reading in a stick-to-your-skin humid bar in a small South Texas town.

We all have the gift of going missing,
like the breath of a collapsing lung,
like a whisper from behind, a shooting star.
Or do we just hide reading a newspaper upside-down
when the new sheriff arrives?

Puede ser que también los periódicos se convierten
lanchas que se lanzan en un río olvidado, en aguas
color a sangre de tantos que casi por las yemas de los dedos
tocaban tierra estadounidense.

The missing,
they recite "Howl" across the Río Grande,
not the Ginsberg lament for his brethren
but the howls of suffering souls crammed in stash houses
across our children's playgrounds, those left
for dead in sweltering sardine packed vessels,
 those left alive to remember hell is real.
Los desaparecidos,
quieren ser encontrados
aun decapitados y sin lenguas.
Siguen gritando porque el silencio es fuerte en sufrimiento.

We will keep them alive and find them!

Through art, poetry, music, stories that scare the night,
and lullabies that make our children sleep tight.

Cuando los cantos se vuelven agua,
el olor de cuchillos en el aire,
bailan con la buganvilla trepadora
descendiéndose seis pies bajo la tierra sin nombre,
solo una alabanza que fluye entre la tierra agrietada.

BREATHING WHILE BROWN

To the Capitol Nine, April 2010, Arizona

ALMA LUZ VILLANUEVA

To the beautiful, brave
young who have always
sat at lunch counters,
racists spitting on them, pulling

their hair, calling them "Nigger,"
killing the brave, young, white
students who joined them—
the insane dogs taking bites of their

tender skin, the insane police who
hose them down, killing pressure,
to their knees, take them to
hot, filthy jails, the ones meant

for Colored—the beautiful,
young Black Panthers, Brown Berets,
hunted into extinction, AIM at
Wounded Knee, Leonard Peltier in

jail more than twenty years, a wise man,
a shaman, after all these years,
knowing the spirit is always, yes,
always, free—Malcolm X,

Mandela knew this, every pregnant
woman knows this, Gandhi
knew this, Aung San Suu Kyi
knows this, the spirit is always, yes,

always, free. I remember my
youngest son followed home
daily in Santa Cruz Califas, Breathing
While Brown. I went to the cop

station and had a fucking fit—
what do we do when an entire
state makes it perfectly legal
to punish humans for Breathing

While Brown—nine young, beautiful
brown warriors chained themselves
to the Capitol's entrance, that's what
we do, the beautiful, brave

young. César Chávez would be
proud. Martin Luther King would be
proud. Gandhi would be
proud. Dolores Huerta is

proud, of the beautiful,
brave young. And my son
continues to breathe while brown,
always free.

ALWAYS HERE

For Arizona and everywhere else

RICH VILLAR

The lack of a proper entrance
into a poem
about Arizona Senate Bill 1070
prompts me instead
to tell you

about the *flamboyanes* blooming
in Doña Yeya's mouth
every time she speaks
about her children,
or the *pasteles* that do not
wrap themselves
until blood is offered to the masa,
or the boys she sent to Germany
who came back headless
and quoting Bible verses,
or the girls
with twenty years of bruises
at the hands of those same boys,
girls who were told *Así es la vida*
without the slightest sense of irony,
who shouldered Nuyorican babies
dutifully to Bayamón
dreaming about a nation
under which they cannot
legally claim citizenship,
or *parrandas* of gold stomping
flat the Jersey snow
forgetting that coquito
never meant cold weather,
or the act of forgetting
beneath every aguinaldo,
because civil *cafecito*
and politics cannot coexist,
and we do not question
our birth certificates
unless we are agents of Homeland Security,

because we were born American citizens
and as such are eligible to die
at a higher rate
in exchange for houses in Jersey
that we do not own.

There are Puerto Ricans
in Arizona and New York and Nebraska,
and I promise you, good *gente*
it makes no difference
if your grandmother conjures
Michoacán or Mayagüez
in her flowered breath;
it makes no difference
if you bless the four winds
or pray to San Juan Bautista:

to those who see only papers
and brown flesh,
who cannot locate your cities
on the maps
of conquerors or conquered,

you are a threat.

And if this is the case,
gente, I say,
be a threat. Unquieted,
bloom where you are not permitted
to bloom. Disjointed,
walk anywhere you please, stumble
if you must, but be present.
And when they ask you
where you keep your company,
tell them here, here,
always here.

MAY DAY IS NOT THE DAY TO SHOOT AT PEOPLE WHO WORK FOR YOU

GEORGE WALLACE

mayday is not the day to shoot at people
who work for you—the ones who do
the work it is beneath you to do—no
not mayday—not the day for vigilante
posses—not the day to catch families
crossing the border or lock them up
in holding tanks and send them back
to their own damn country—not on
mayday we do not beat men outside
train stations today ladies and gents
nor do we drag them behind cars
—and we do not leave them bleeding
behind latino bars today—no sir!
we do not sneer at shift workers who
pack food in refrigerated trucks or
insult the women behind counters
at fast food joints no not today—
the ones who wash plates set our
tables wait on us in slick friendly
fashionable downtown restaurants
serving empanadas plantain chips
black bean soup guacamole dip
and margaritas no not on mayday
—we do not demonize the ones
who do the work we have no
inclination to do—the jobs our
parents or grandparents did to
put us through college—may
day is the day we honor those
who tend to the lawns we gaze
out upon on sunday morning
as we prepare to thank and to
praise the sweet lord who made
us all, for the many blessings of
being rich and american—dish
washers busboys warehouse
workers housemaids carpenters

tin can fillers crab shell shellers
pea pickers potato peelers street
sweepers today is the day for
them—no we do not write hate
mail to politicians today or carry
placards or call in to call-in radio
station talk show hosts—nor do
we give fictitious names and rage
and rant we do not make speeches
or pass laws pandering to the people
who write hate mail—no not on
mayday we don't—mayday is the
day of the able-bodied workers who
sweat and sway inside buses and vans
—who slave in kitchens and ride on
the backs of pickups and dump trucks
—the day for those who are unafraid
of honest work for minimum pay—

men who bend down and whisper secrets
into our pregnant soil

women who scrub our toilets at night

SESTINA FOR ILLEGAL WIDOWS*

LORI A. WILLIAMS

Luz tries to get some papers together.
The blonde lady at the Red Cross promises to help,
get her some sort of aid, with proof that her Pedro
worked for Fine & Schapiro in the Trade Towers;
delivered breakfast and lunch to the women and men
whose families grieve and rage, but always eat

enough. Her three young children miss eating
the food papa once brought home—burgers and ice cream—together
at a big basement table full of cousins, uncles, aunts, women and men
with golden smiles for their American dream. The help
was what they were called, cleaning the restrooms in the towers,
washing dishes in delis, delivering corned beef and salad, like Pedro

did, six days a week. His tips were big. You are my best worker, Pedro,
his boss Miguel said, and Luz was so proud. Now come eat
at my table, let's talk! I see you moving on to waiter. These towers,
they make men like us rich! We must stick together
in this free and prosperous land. With this money, we help
our families back home, prove we are able men.

Luz and her friends have lost many good, strong men
to this free, safe, rich country. Manuel and Pedro
were brothers, six kids between them. The women help
each other with rice and beans and plantains to eat,
cheap, plentiful, but never enough. They cry and fret together
for their loves and tomorrow. After the fall of the towers,

family back home kept asking long distance, where did the towers
go? Luz tried to explain what she didn't understand. Our men
are gone, mama. There is nothing to send you! Hands together

---

*Author's note: I wrote this one after reading about the plight of the families of all the
undocumented immigrant workers at the WTC. Most of them were deliverymen, working at the
restaurants on the concourse level. There are no numbers as to how many of them died . . . because
most of them were not citizens, yet . . . they worked hard and supported their families here and in
Mexico. I remember reading an article about their wives and children and how they were lost. . . .
no income, nowhere to turn. This is for them.

in prayer, the parents spoke to God—where is our Manuel? Our Pedro?
Candles were lit, town square filled with fear. How will we live, eat
without them? How can we bury not even a bone? God, help!

Luz finds no proof. Only clucks of regret, no help
from blondes or any other saviors. Money in the towers'
fund is not for her kind—those who came to America to eat
three meals a day with kids and anxious limbs. Hardworking men
who toiled in kitchens and bathrooms and carried lunch sacks, like Pedro,
to offer their families a dream: to succeed as a people, together

in New York, where there is no help for families without papers. Men
employed in the towers, who died with our own, like Pedro,
leave wives like Luz, scrounging to eat, to live, to be acknowledged—
together.

DIASPORA

"The voice of thy brother's blood crieth unto me from the ground."
—from the Book of Genesis 4:10

MEG WITHERS

Constant leave-taking
become now an art.
Displaced cards in a deck
shuffled over and over
in the hands of an
excuse for God.

Flocks
of white and black birds
landing in a blast of new land.
Seagulls and crows, pulsing
necks in and out,
searching this new place
for evidence
of water.

Setting up cloth and skin tents,
abraded by drier air.
Unfurled,
flooring, seating, bedding
comes to rest,
long before bodies
will sit and pace and pray
and finally sleep on them.
Settle at dark,
so many
lanterns of red blood,
in a new corner of night.

Home is here,
and then there
and there,
a word filled with echoes,
hollow emptied oil jars
that once fed multitudes.
Dry eyes are
late summer riverbeds,
burdened by dispossession.

Rivers once flooded yearly,
now arid—but for blood.
Dispossessed supplications
bounce unheard
off military ears,
gods manipulate justice
with new weapons.

In the dry, white wind,
bellies of tents
undulate and sigh,
a child sits at a tent peg,
tan nostrils furling.

The scent of Cain,
greedy landowner.
Rife here with milky
redolence of cut barley,
dispelling odors of
Abel's flocks—
repeating and repeating
this unacceptable,
lamblike sacrifice.

WE ARE THE ONES WE HAVE BEEN WAITING FOR

STEPHANIE YAN

We are the ones we have been waiting for
though no one waits for us
silently striving on an empty shore
holding on and fighting for a tomorrow
under the long shadow cast by June
strategically surrendering to the status quo
The flash and flare of fall came and went too soon
we are scattered soldier seeds
December comes and finds us alone
some have sprouted some are bruised
some have kept on keeping on the tasks and deeds
despite the inner dangers and demons loose
In the dark singularly each by each
we work to find the music track
so the mute in us can regain our song and speech
clamoring quietly for the words to come back because
we are the ones we have been waiting for

WHY I FEEL THE WAY I DO ABOUT SB 1070

"If the hurt in someone else hurts us, in a man
we don't know, who is
present always and is the victim
and the enemy and love and all
we need to be whole."
—*from "The Other," by Rosario Castellanos*

ANDRE YANG

Because my fifth grade teacher, Mr. Sánchez,
compared my future to gold. Because
when I told my friend Ernesto
about an uncle's three-day funeral,
he told me about his grandmother's three-day funeral.
Because of what Christianity has done
for me. Because there is corruption
in all organizations. Because we're all victims
of colonialism. Because
when the first girl I thought I loved
didn't feel the same way back,
Tommy Bernal surprised me with the first hug
I'd ever received from a friend.
Because no one else hugged me
again for another three years. Because
Sherman Alexie recognizes that the Hmong
are the Native Americans of Asia. Because
John Doe Xiong is suing the United States
for the right to go back to Laos
to die with his family on land he still calls
home. Because there are still
animals like the saola that, when forced
behind walls, would prefer death. Because
I've read about the Native American man
who, the last of his tribe, refused to give
his name to the white remains
of humanity. Because indigenous peoples
are closer to the land and its spirits
and in being so are closer to one
another no matter where they are
in the world. Because SB 1070 is hate
manifested on paper in words. Because I

believed for too long that I couldn't do anything
about anything. Because a girl named Rosa
once kissed my cheek. Because I have not forgotten
what it means to "love thy neighbor." Because
my cousin, Virus, never acquired
citizenship, was convicted of manslaughter
after a gang fight, spent six years in
an Arizona prison, and is on parole release
pending deportation once U.S.-Laos relations improve.
Because no one stood up for my people
when they needed the help. Because the Hmong,
running for their lives in the jungles of Laos,
still need help. Because America
fucked things up in Vietnam, the Secret War,
the Middle East, and is desperate to prove
it knows how to finish something.

CONTRIBUTORS

Francisco X. Alarcón is a Chicano poet, educator, and author of twelve volumes of poetry, including *From the Other Side of Night: Selected and New Poems*. His most recent books are *Canto hondo / Deep Songs* and *Borderless Butterflies / Mariposas sin fronteras*. He founded the Facebook page "Poets Responding to SB 1070" and teaches at University of California, Davis.

JoAnn Anglin, a member of Los Escritores del Nuevo Sol (Writers of the New Sun), has a chapbook, *Words Like Knives, Like Feathers* (Rattlesnake Press), and poems in *The Sacramento Anthology: One Hundred Poems, Tule Review, Rattlesnake Review, The Pagan Muse*, and *Voces del Nuevo Sol*.

Francisco Aragón is the author of *Puerta del Sol* and *Glow of Our Sweat*, as well as the editor of the award-winning anthology *The Wind Shifts: New Latino Poetry*. He directs Letras Latinas, the literary program of the Institute for Latino Studies at the University of Notre Dame.

Cathy Arellano, poet, author, educator, and activist, has a published chapbook, *I Love My Women, Sometimes They Love Me*. She has written a collection of stories about San Francisco's Mission District called *Flats and Bars* and is editing *Homegrown: A Cultural Microhistory of Latinos in the Mission*. She has had works published in *Huizache* and *The Malpaís Review*.

Jorge Tetl Argueta is a poet from El Salvador who now lives in San Francisco. He is the author of many award-winning children's books, among them *A Movie in My Pillow, Sopa de frijoles / Bean Soup*, and *Arroz con leche / Rice Pudding*. He is director of Talleres de Poesía, a literary organization that promotes children's literature in the United States and El Salvador.

Adrián Arias, a poet and artist originally from Peru, has resided in California since 2000. One of his pieces was awarded "best poem" at the 2009 International Poetry Festival's poetry night in Struga, Macedonia. His multimedia visual work "Beautiful Trash" was featured at San Francisco's de Young Museum in 2010, Galería de la Raza in 2012, and Museo de San Marcos, Lima, Peru, in 2015.

Victor Ávila is an award-winning poet. One of his poems was included in the anthology *Overthrowing Capitalism*. He has written and illustrated several comic books, most recently *Hollywood Ghost Comix Vol. 2*, published by Ghoula Press. Victor has taught in California public schools for twenty-five years.

Avotcja is a card-carrying New York–born music fanatic/sound junkie and popular Bay Area radio deejay. She's a lifelong musician/writer/educator and is on a shamelessly spirit-driven melodic mission to heal herself. Avotcja talks to the trees and listens to the wind against the concrete, and when they answer it usually winds up in a poem.

Devreaux Baker has published three books of poetry; her most recent book is *Out of the Bones of Earth*. She is the recipient of a PEN Oakland Josephine Miles poetry award for *Red Willow People*, a 2012 Women's Global Leadership Poetry Award, and a Hawaii Council of Humanities Poetry Award.

Kristopher Barney is a Diné (Navajo) farmer, rancher, artist, activist, and writer from the community of Rough Rock in the Navajo Nation. He has published nationally and internationally about the love he has for his homeland and his people. He works to defend the sacred and all life.

Virginia Barrett is a poet and artist whose books include *I Just Wear My Wings: Collected Poems of an Aspiring Mystic* and *Singing My Naked Lines: North Beach Poems*. She is also the editor of two anthologies of contemporary San Francisco poets, *Feather Floating on the Water: Poems for Our Children* and *OCCUPY SF: Poems from the Movement* (with Bobby Coleman).

Esmeralda Bernal was born in Raymondville, Texas; spent the major part of her life in California; and currently resides in Phoenix, Arizona. Her poetry has appeared in *Yellow Medicine Review*, *Nahualliandoing*, the *Journal of MALCS*, and *San Gabriel Quarterly Review*.

Sarah Browning is cofounder and executive director of Split This Rock and an associate fellow of the Institute for Policy Studies. Author of *Whiskey in the Garden of Eden* and coeditor of *DC Poets Against the War: An Anthology*, she has written essays that have appeared in *Utne Reader*, *Foreign Policy in Focus*, *On the Issues*, and *Sojourners*.

Carmen Calatayud's book of poems *In the Company of Spirits* was a runner-up for the Walt Whitman Award, given by the Academy of American Poets. She is a Larry Neal Poetry Award winner, a *La Bloga* Best Poem of 2013 winner, and a Virginia Center for the Creative Arts fellow. She is a poetry moderator for "Poets Responding to SB 1070." Born to a Spanish father and Irish mother in the United States, she works and writes in Washington, DC.

Xánath Caraza is the author of *Sílabas de viento / Syllables of Wind* (2014), *Noche de colibríes: Ekphrastic Poems* (2014), *Lo que trae la marea / What the Tide Brings* (2013), *Conjuro* (2012) and *Corazón Pintado: Ekphrastic Poems* (2012). She writes the column "U.S. Latino Poets *en español*" for *La Bloga*. She is a member of the Advisory Circle of Con Tinta, a collective of Chican@/Latin@ Activist Writers. She teaches at University of Missouri—Kansas City.

Héctor Carbajal is a visiting assistant professor at DePaul University. He has a BA in English and an MA in borderlands history. In 2010, he earned a PhD in rhetoric and writing studies at University of Texas at El Paso. His writing has been featured in *This Bridge We Call Home: Radical Visions for Transformation*, which was a Lambda Literary Award finalist.

Elizabeth Cazassús, poet and performance artist from Tijuana, Mexico, is the author of nine books of poems. Her most recent books are *No es mentira este paraíso* (2009), *Enediana* (2010), *Razones de la dama infiel* (2012), and *Hijas de la ira* (2013). She is a teacher and also edits and writes for a cultural section of *El Sol de Tijuana*. She is a recipient of several literary awards for her poetry, which has been translated into English and Polish.

Lorna Dee Cervantes is a major Mexican American poet whose works have achieved national recognition. Her first book, *Emplumada* (1981), was a recipient of the American Book Award. Her second collection, *From the Cables of Genocide: Poems on Love and Hunger* (1991), received many literary awards. She received a Pulitzer nomination for *Drive: The First Quartet*. Her most recent books are *Ciento: 100 100-Word Love Poems* and *Sueño*, both from Wing Press.

Ana Chig is a Mexican poet born in Los Mochis, Sinaloa, and currently living in Tijuana, Baja California. She is the editor of the monthly poetry journal *Frontera-Esquina: Revista Mensual de Poesía*, which is published in Tijuana. She has organized several poetry festivals involving U.S. Chicano/Latino poets and Mexican poets in the San Diego/Tijuana border region.

Jabez W. Churchill was born in Northern California and educated in California and Argentina. He teaches Spanish at Santa Rosa Junior College and Mendocino College. He's been a California poet in the public schools since 1998, has been a political activist since 1969, and began submitting poetry for publication in 1979.

Antoinette Nora Claypoole moved from the East Coast to Ashland, Oregon, in the early 1980s, where she met members of the American Indian Movement (AIM). Her work with AIM informs her writing life. Founding editor of Wild Embers Press, she has completed a biography of the radical journalist Louise Bryant, *Flower of Bronze: The Lost Stories of Louise Bryant* (1885–1936), for which she received an Oregon Literary Arts Award.

Karen S. Córdova lives in California, but has deep roots in Colorado and New Mexico. Her poetry often reflects love of her heritage and concern for social issues. She participates in readings as a featured poet. Her first book, *Pass the Farolito*, was released in 2013.

Iris De Anda is a writer, activist, and practitioner of the healing arts. A native of Los Angeles of Mexican and Salvadoran descent, she believes in the power of spoken word, poetry, storytelling, and dreams. Her latest book of poems is *Codeswith: Fires from Mi Corazón*. Her poems have appeared in the *Mujeres de Maíz Zine, OCCUPY SF: Poems from the Movement, Seeds of Resistance, In the Words of Women,* and *Twenty: In Memoriam.*

Nephtalí De León is a former migrant worker with no formal education beyond high school. He is the author of *Chican@s: Our Background and Our Pride, Chicano Popcorn, I Will Catch the Sun,* and *Poemas de la Resistencia Chicana* (in Catalan and Chicano Caló). His poetry has been translated into Russian, Arabic, and Chinese. He is the creator of the movie *La Llorona.*

Susan Deer Cloud is a Catskill Mountain Indian. Recipient of a National Endowment for the Arts Literature Fellowship and of two New York State Foundation for the Arts Poetry Fellowships, she has had work published in numerous journals and anthologies. Her most recent books are *Hunger Moon, Fox Mountain, Braiding Starlight, Car Stealer,* and *The Last Ceremony.*

Elena Díaz Björkquist is a writer and an artist from Tucson, Arizona. Elena is the author of *Suffer Smoke* and *Water from the Moon* and coeditor of *Sowing the Seeds: Una cosecha de recuerdos* and *Our Spirit, Our Reality: Celebrating Our Stories*, anthologies by Sowing the Seeds, a collective of women writers. Elena was a moderator of the Facebook page "Poets Responding to SB 1070."

James Downs recently retired as associate editor of Poetic Matrix Press, which published his chapbook, *Where Manzanita*, and a full volume, *Merge with the River*. He has a budding song lyricist career; is a loving stepfather and grandfather to his dear wife Joy's daughters and grandsons; and he digs his cats, Belle de Bayou and Angel. James lives in a paradise called Yosemite National Park and also has a home in Sonora, both in the beloved Sierra Nevada Mountains.

Qwo-Li Driskill is a Cherokee two-spirit poet, activist, and performer. S/he is the author of *Walking with Ghosts: Poems* and the coeditor of *Queer Indigenous Studies: Critical Interventions in Theory, Politics, and Literature* and *Sovereign Erotics: A Collection of Two-Spirit Literature*. S/he is an assistant professor of queer studies at Oregon State University.

Sharon Doubiago's memoir, *My Father's Love*, volume 1, *Portrait of the Poet as a Young Girl*, was a finalist in the Northern California Book Awards in Creative Non Fiction in 2010. She has published more than a hundred essays, from the personal and creative to the scholarly, and has recently completed *Naked to the Earth*, a poetry manuscript.

Sharon Elliott was born and raised in Seattle. She has written since childhood. She served four years in the Peace Corps in Nicaragua and Ecuador, which laid the foundation for her activism. As an initiated Lucumi priest, she has learned about her ancestral Scottish history, reinforcing her belief that borders are created by men and that enforcing them is simply wrong. She has a book of poems, *Jaguar Unfinished* (2012).

Mario Ángel Escobar is a U.S.-Salvadoran writer and poet, founder and editor of Izote Press. In 2006, Escobar won political asylum, making him one of the few Salvadorans to do so after the Peace Accords of 1992. His poetry collections include *Al correr de las horas*, *Gritos interiores*, *La Nueva Tendencia*, and *Paciente*. He currently lives in Alhambra, California.

Martín Espada has published more than fifteen books. His forthcoming collection of poems is called *The Leaves of El Moriviví* (2016). *The Republic of Poetry* (2006) was a finalist for the Pulitzer Prize. His honors include the Shelley Memorial Award and a Guggenheim Fellowship. His book of essays, *Zapata's Disciple* (1998), was banned in Tucson as part of the Mexican American studies program outlawed by the State of Arizona. He teaches at the University of Massachusetts Amherst.

Odilia Galván Rodríguez, eco-poet, writer, editor, and activist, is the author of five volumes of poetry, her latest, *The Nature of Things*, along with photographer Richard Loya. She was the English edition editor of *Tricontinental Magazine* in Havana, Cuba. She facilitates creative writing workshops nationally and is a moderator of "Poets Responding to SB 1070" and "Love and Prayers for Fukushima," both Facebook pages dedicated to bringing attention to social justice issues that affect the lives and well-being of many people.

Daniel García Ordaz, from McAllen, Texas, is a teacher at Weslaco East High School, founder of the Rio Grande Valley International Poetry Festival, and the author of *You Know What I'm Sayin'?* García has been featured in Texas Latino Voices and the Dallas International Book Fair. He appears in *Altar: Cruzando fronteras / Building Bridges*, a documentary about Gloria Anzaldúa.

Nancy Aidé González is a Chicana poet, educator, and activist who lives in Lodi, California. Her work has appeared in *Huizache: The Magazine of Latino Literature*, *La Tolteca*, *Mujeres De Maíz Zine*, *Dove Tales*, *Tule Review*, *Seeds of Resistance Flor y Canto: Tortilla Warrior*, *Hinchas de Poesía*, *La Bloga*, and several literary anthologies. She is a participating member of Escritores del Nuevo Sol.

Sonia Gutiérrez, a promoter of social justice, teaches English at Palomar College in San Marcos, California. Her poetry and vignettes have appeared in *La Bloga, Contratiempo, CRATE, El Tecolote, Mujeres de Maíz, Fringe Magazine*, and *Huizache. Spider Woman / La mujer araña* (2013) is her bilingual poetry collection. *Kissing Dreams from a Distance*, a novel, is under editorial review. Sonia is at work on *Legacy / Herencia*, a book of poetry.

Israel Francisco Haros López is both a visual artist and a performance artist. He was born in East Los Angeles, received his BA in English, and earned an MFA in writing from California College of the Arts. His poetry explores contemporary Xikan@ border politics and searches for indigenous spiritual truths using trilingual experiments. Among the books he has published are *Waterhummingbirdhouse: A Chicano Poetry Codex* and *Xikanada: A Xikano Sacred Geometry Codex*.

Gabriel Hartley is an English professor in Athens, Ohio. He and his wife, Anna Oksanen, spend a good deal of time journeying with the nature spirits and other entities in their woods there and at sacred sites around the world.

Ralph Haskins was born and raised in Monterrey, Mexico. His family moved to South Texas during the social turmoil of the 1960s. Many of his poems touch on the cultural and political issues of our times. Today, Ralph lives in McAllen, Texas, where he supplements his poet's income by moonlighting as a science teacher at a local high school.

Claudia D. Hernández was born and raised in Guatemala. She is the founder of Today's Revolutionary Women of Color Project. Her photography, poetry, and prose have been published in *La Tolteca, Hinchas de Poesía*, "Poets Responding to SB 1070," *La Bloga, Texas Poetry Calendar 2014*, the *Journal of MALCS, The Mom Egg Review*, and the *Berkeley Poetry Review*, among others.

Andrea Hernández Holm was born and raised in Arizona. Her heart is happiest in the desert, and her writing is rooted there. She is a graduate student in Mexican American studies, a former moderator for "Poets Responding to SB 1070," and a comadre of the Sowing the Seeds writing collective.

Juan Felipe Herrera was a longtime citizen of La Mission (since 1950) and has worked on various cultural arts projects in the San Francisco Bay Area. Herrera is a winner of the 2009 National Book Critics Circle Award and a 2010 Guggenheim Fellowship. He teaches in the Department of Creative Writing at the University of California, Riverside. In 2012 he was named Poet Laureate of California. He is the present U.S. Poet Laureate and lives in Fresno, California.

Mari Herreras is a fifth-generation Tucsonan and proud to be a poet who never uses the term *Nazizona* to describe her beloved, albeit troubled, state. When Herreras isn't writing for the *Tucson Weekly* or composing poetry, she explores Tucson and life with her son, whom she credits with saving her soul.

Susana de Jesús Huerta was born and raised in the San Francisco Bay Area. She has taught English writing and literature at all levels from middle school to college and currently teaches composition and literature at Foothill College. Suzy is an alumna of VONA/Voices. Her poetry has appeared on *La Bloga, El Coraje*, "Poets Responding to SB 1070," *Sunrise from Blue Thunder*, and the *Packinghouse Review*.

Aurora Levins Morales is a Puerto Rican Jewish feminist writer, historian, visual artist, and activist. She is the author of *Remedios: Stories of Earth and Iron from the History of Puertorriqueñas* and *Medicine Stories, Kindling: Writings on the Body* and has coauthored two books with her mother, Rosario Morales, *Getting Home Alive* and *Cosecha and Other Stories*. Her work has been widely anthologized and has been translated into seven languages.

Genny Lim has been a featured poet at world poetry festivals in Venezuela; Sarajevo, Bosnia and Herzegovina; and Naples, Italy. She has four poetry collections, *Winter Place, Child of War, Paper Gods and Rebels*, and *From Both Shores*; has edited an anthology of Japanese and Chinese women's family memoirs; and is coauthor of *Island: Poetry and History of Chinese Immigrants on Angel Island*, which received the American Book Award.

Mark Lipman is the author of six books, most recently *Poetry for the Masses* and *Global Economic Amnesty*. Cofounder of the Berkeley Stop the War Coalition (USA), Agir Contre la Guerre (France), and Occupy Los Angeles, he has been an outspoken critic of war and occupation since 2001. He's currently a member of Occupy Venice and the Revolutionary Poets Brigade.

César Love is a native of Northern California and a Latino poet influenced by the Asian masters. His book of poems is titled *While Bees Sleep*. An editor of the *Haight Ashbury Literary Journal*, he is also building a bridge between the poets of the San Francisco Bay Area and the poets of Mérida, Yucatán.

Manuel Lozano, self-taught writer and artist, lives in El Paso, "El Chuco," Texas, cradle of the pachuco. Manuel writes traditional verse "to the rhythm of the Matachines." His work has appeared in *Xican@ Poetry Daily* and *La Bloga*. To purchase *Seeds of Rebellion*, visit his blog, *Manuel Lozano: Xicano Writing*.

Devorah Major is a California-born granddaughter of immigrants, documented and undocumented, who served as San Francisco's Third Poet

Laureate (2002–2006). She has published four poetry books, two novels, two biographies, and a host of short stories, essays, and individual poems. Her most recent poetry book is *Teardrops in the Mouth of the Moon*. She has served as poet in residence at the Fine Arts Museums of San Francisco and as a part-time adjunct professor at California College of the Arts. She is also an iterant member of the International Revolutionary Poets Brigade.

Andrea García Mauk grew up in Arizona. She writes poetry, fiction, screenplays, and stage plays and teaches theater. Her work has been featured on *The Late, Late Show with Tom Snyder* and in *Victorian Homes Magazine*, the anthology *Our Spirit, Our Reality*, the *Mujeres de Maíz Zine*, and *Hinchas de Poesía*. She lives in Los Angeles.

Joseph McNair has written four books of poetry and one novel based on the Ifa-Orisha world view, called *Ose Shango*. He has a black music history book, *I Hear Music in the Air*, forthcoming.

John Martínez has had several poems published in *La Bloga*. As a musician/political activist/poet he has performed with Teatro de La Tierra, Los Perros del Pueblo, and TROKA, a Poetry Ensemble (lead by poet Juan Felipe Herrera). He has toured with several *cumbia* bands throughout California's Central Valley and Los Angeles.

Octaviano Merecias-Cuevas is a trilingual Mixtec poet, sociolinguist, researcher, filmmaker, and community educator. He has provided mentoring and guidance to youth and families in Mexico and the United States. His poetry has appeared in *Prism*, *El Tecolote*, and *La Bloga*. He has taught bilingual poetry at Ethos Music Center, *centro cultural* of Washington County, in Oregon.

James O. Michael, although born in a monolingual English-speaking culture, learned Spanish in college, married a young woman from Chihuahua, México, and became a teacher of Spanish and ESL. After retiring, he joined Los Escritores del Nuevo Sol, a group in Sacramento, California, that inspires him to write in Spanish and in English.

Edith Morris-Vásquez was born in El Paso, Texas, and grew up in the Beaumont/Cherry Valley community of California, where she and her six siblings attended public school. She went on to receive academic degrees at the University of California in both Los Angeles and Riverside.

Yasmeen Najmi's *querencia* is as wide and long as the old Río Grande. She is an environmental planner and public servant, and the river seeps and shapes her life and language. Her poems have appeared in the *As Us Journal*, *Graffiti Kolkata Broadside*, *Artistica*, *La Bloga*, *El Tecolote's 40th Anniversary Literary Edition*, *Poets for Living Waters*, and the anthologies *The Stark Electric*

Space, Adobe Walls, and *Fixed and Free Poetry.* She lives in Albuquerque's North Valley.

Joe Navarro is a literary *vato loco,* teacher, poet, creative writer, husband, father, and grandfather. Joe integrates his poetic voice with life's experiences and blends culture with politics. His poetic influences include the Beat poets, the Last Poets, Amiri Baraka, Sonia Sanchez, Alurista, Gloria Anzaldúa, Lalo Delgado, and numerous others.

Gerardo Pacheco Matus migrated to the United States at fifteen years of age. Pacheco's Mayan and Mexican heritage influences his writing, which deals with immigration and the social and cultural hardships his immigrant and undocumented community has to struggle against in this country.

Melinda Palacio's chapbook, *Folsom Lockdown,* won Kulupi Press's Sense of Place prize in 2009. Her novel, *Ocotillo Dreams,* received the PEN Oakland Josephine Miles Award and the Mariposa Award at the International Latino Book Festival. Her poetry collection, *How Fire Is a Story, Waiting,* was a finalist for the Milt Kessler and the Patterson Prizes and received first prize in poetry at the 2013 International Latino Book Awards. In 2014, she was a finalist for the Rita Dove Poetry Prize and for the the William Faulkner– William Wisdom Creative Writing Competition. She writes a regular column for *La Bloga.*

Carlos Parada Ayala coedited the poetry anthology *Al pie de la Casa Blanca: Poetas hispanos de Washington, DC* (2010) and is the author of the poetry book *La luz de la tormenta* (2013).

Ramón Piñero is an ex–San Francisco Bay Area poet living in the buckle of the Bible Belt, aka Florida, where good little boys and girls grow up to be Republicans and vote against their own interests. He's the father of three and grandfather to six of the coolest kids ever. His poetry has been published in *La Bloga.*

Manuel Ramos, author of eight novels, is a cofounder of and regular contributor to *La Bloga,* a blog devoted to literature, news, and opinion. Recent publications: *Desperado: A Mile High Noir* (2013), *King of the Chicanos* (2010), and the short story collection *The Skull of Pancho Villa, and Other Stories* (2015).

Maritza Rivera a Puerto Rican poet who lived in Tucson, Arizona, when SB 1070 was passed. She is the publisher of Casa Mariposa Press, creator of a short form of poetry called Blackjack, and the author of *About You, A Mother's War, Baker's Dozen,* and *Twenty-One: Blackjack Poems.*

Margarita Robleda, born in Mérida, Yucatán, grew up visiting her grandparents in San Antonio, Texas. That is why she introduces herself as, "I'm bilingual, bicultural, but most of all, by heart!" She is the author of 115 books for children published in Mexico, Colombia, and the United States, where some are included in bilingual education programs.

Roberto Cintli Rodríguez is a longtime award-winning journalist and columnist who returned to school in 2003 in pursuit of a master's degree (2005) and a PhD in mass communications (2008) at the University of Wisconsin—Madison. He teaches at the University of Arizona and is the author of *Our Sacred Maíz Is Our Mother: Indigeneity and Belonging in the Americas*.

Renato Rosaldo's first poetry collection, *Prayer to Spider Woman / Rezo a la mujer araña*, won the American Book Award. His second book, *Diego Luna's Insider Tips*, won the Many Mountains Moving Poetry Book Manuscript Prize, selected by Martín Espada. His most recent book of poetry, *The Day of Shelly's Death*, was published by Duke University Press in 2014. As a cultural anthropologist, he is the author of *Culture and Truth*.

Gabriel Rosenstock, born 1949 in postcolonial Ireland, is a poet, haikuist, novelist, essayist, and playwright. Author-translator of more than 180 books, mostly in Irish (Gaelic), he is a member of Aosdána (the Irish Academy of Arts & Letters) and a lineage holder of Celtic Buddhism.

Joseph Ross is the author of two poetry collections, *Gospel of Dust* (2013) and *Meeting Bone Man* (2012). Twice nominated for a Pushcart Prize, he has had his poems published in many anthologies, including *Collective Brightness: LGBTIQ Poets on Faith, Religion, and Spirituality*. His poems have appeared in many journals and other periodicals, including the *Los Angeles Times*, *Poet Lore*, and *Tidal Basin Review*.

Abel Salas is a Los Angeles journalist and poet whose works have appeared in the *New York Times*, *Los Angeles Magazine*, the *Los Angeles Times*, *ZYZZYVA*, *Huizache*, and the *Austin Chronicle*, among others. He has taught poetry in LA juvenile halls and at Corazón del Pueblo, a community arts center in the East Los Angeles barrio of Boyle Heights. He is the publisher and editor of *Brooklyn & Boyle*. He has participated in poetry festivals in the United States, Mexico, and Cuba.

Raúl Sánchez is a poet and translator currently working on the Spanish version of his collection *All Our Brown-Skinned Angels*, which was nominated for the 2013 Washington State Book Award in poetry. He was one of the twelve 2014 Jack Straw Writers and one of the mentors and judges for the 2014 Poetry on Buses project sponsored by 4 Culture and

King County Metro in Washington. He lives in Seattle and conducts workshops on the Day of the Dead.

Matt Sedillo is a two-time national slam poet champion, grand slam champion of the Damn Slam Los Angeles 2011, and the author of *For What I Might Do Tomorrow*, published by Caza de Poesia in 2010. His poetry has been published in anthologies alongside works by the likes of such literary giants as Amiri Baraka, Lawrence Ferlinghetti, Jack Hirschman, and Luis Rodríguez.

Nina Serrano is a poet, educator, and independent media producer. *Heart Strong: Selected Poems, 2000–2012* won the PEN Oakland Josephine Miles Award in 2014. *Heart's Journey: Selected Poems, 1980–1999* won the Artists International Embassy Award for best book in 2013. Her first book, *Heart Songs: Collected Poems of Nina Serrano, 1969–1980* was first published by Editorial Pocho-Che. Nina produces "La Raza Chronicles" at KPFA-FM in Berkeley, California.

Tom Sheldon's artwork has been shown in local galleries, as well as the New Mexico Museum of Natural History and Science in Albuquerque. He has won art competitions at the state fair level. He also loves to write poetry and has been published in *La Bloga*, the e-magazine *Monique's Passions*, "Poets Responding to SB 1070" on Facebook, and *Writers in the Storm*.

Hedy García Treviño is a Chicana poet and artist from New Mexico who currently lives in Phoenix, Arizona. Her work has been published in numerous journals and publications and she has participated in many poetry readings. She is one of the active moderators of "Poets Responding to SB 1070," where she has published more than forty of her own poems.

Tara Evonne Trudell studied film, audio, and photography while in college at New Mexico Highlands University. She is a recent graduate with her BFA in media arts. Incorporating poetry, she addresses the many troubling issues that are ongoing in society and hopes that her works will create an emotional impact that inspires others to act.

Luis Alberto Urrea, born in Tijuana, Mexico, to a Mexican father and American mother, has published extensively in all major genres. He is the author of thirteen books, among them *The Devils Highway* (2004), which won the Lannan Literary Award and was a finalist for the Pulitzer Prize, *The Hummingbird's Daughter* (2006), and *Into the Beautiful North* (2010). He is a professor of creative writing at the University of Illinois at Chicago.

Pamela Uschuk is editor in chief of the literary magazine *Cutthroat: A Journal of the Arts* and lives in Bayfield, Colorado. She was featured writer at the 2011 and 2013 Prague Summer Programs as well as at the 2011 Sha'ar

Writers Conference in Tel Aviv. In 2011, Uschuk was the John C. Hodges Visiting Writer at University of Tennesee, Knoxville.

Norma Liliana Valdez is an alumna of the VONA/Voices writing workshop, the writing program at University of California, Berkeley, Extension, and a 2014 Hedgebrook writer in residence. Her poems have appeared in *Calyx Journal*, *The Acentos Review*, *As It Ought to Be*, *La Bloga*, and *Dismantle: An Anthology of Writing from the VONA/Voices Writing Workshop*. She lives and works in the San Francisco Bay Area.

Richard Vargas graduated from the University of New Mexico creative writing MFA program in 2010. He has had two books published, *McLife* and *American Jesus*. The Taos Summer Writer's Conference awarded him its 2011 Hispanic Writers Award. He also edits and publishes an independent poetry magazine, *The Más Tequila Review*.

Carlos Vázquez Segura is a Mexican poet and thinker, born in Guadalajara, Jalisco, always in permanent search of essences, images, and metaphors. He has published three books of poems, *Soplos y pensamientos*, *Quijotes y luciérnagas*, and, most recently, *El eco de la piel*, in 2013. He is has a degree in civil engineering from the Universidad ITESO and a master's in business administration from Universidad Panamericana Campus Guadalajara.

Edward A. Vidaurre has been published in several anthologies and literary journals, among them *La Tolteca* zine, *Bordersenses*, *Interstice*, *La Noria Literary Journal*, and the *Boundless* anthology of the Rio Grande Valley International Poetry Festival, 2011–2013. He has had two books published, *I Took My Barrio on a Road Trip* (2013) and *Insomnia* (2014).

Alma Luz Villanueva is the author of seven books of poetry, most recently *Planet*, *Desire*, and *Soft Chaos*. *Planet* won the Latin American Writers Institute Award, and a poem from *Desire* was chosen for *The Best American Poetry* series. Some poems from *Soft Chaos*, as well as poems and fiction from her other books, have been published in anthologies and textbooks. A new book of poetry, *Gracias*, came out in the spring of 2015. And her fourth novel, *Song of the Golden Scorpion*, was published in 2013.

Rich Villar is a writer, editor, activist, and educator originally from Paterson, New Jersey. His first book, *Comprehending Forever*, was published in 2014 by Willow Books. His poems and essays have appeared in *Black Renaissance Noire*, *Radius*, *Union Station*, and *Beltway Poetry Quarterly*. He has been quoted on Latino/a literature and culture by HBO, the *New York Times*, and the *New York Daily News*; his poetry has been featured on NPR's *Latino USA*. He served as the director and curator of Acentos, a grassroots project fostering the Latino/a voice in American letters.

George Wallace is an American poet of celebration and witness. Writer in residence at the Walt Whitman Birthplace, he's stood with Cindy Sheehan, Poets Against the War and Occupy Wall Street and has read or lectured at the Woody Guthrie Festival, Lowell Celebrates Kerouac!, the Steinbeck Center, the Robert Burns Centre, and the Dylan Thomas Centre.

Lori A. Williams passed away in 2013. Her poems were published in dozens of print and online publications, most recently in *Symmetry Pebbles* and *Spiracle Journal*, and she was the first American poet featured on the blog *Poets United: I Wish I'd Written This*. Her first chapbook, *Woman on the Brink*, was published in December 2011 by erbacce-press.

Meg Withers has two published books of poetry: *Must Be Present to Win* and *A Communion of Saints*. She is the poetry editor the photo/poetic art book *Shadowed: Unheard Voices*, published by The Press at Fresno State (2014). Her work has been nationally anthologized and published by a wide range of literary journals. She teaches English and creative writing at Merced Community College.

Stephanie Yan has a BA in development studies from University of California, Berkeley, and an MD from University of California, Davis, surgery residency. "June Jordan made me believe that I am a poet AND I can be a doctor. When she died, I felt lost. This is my first attempt at poetry in remembrance of her and to win myself back."

Andre Yang lives in Fresno, California. He is a founding member of the Hmong American Writers' Circle. He received his creative writing MFA from California State University, Fresno, and currently teaches English at Fresno State and Fresno City College. Andre is a Kundiman Asian American Poetry Fellow and has been awarded an artist's residency at the Ucross Foundation. His poetry has appeared in *Paj Ntaub Voice*, *Lantern Review*, and *Beltway Poetry Quarterly*.